COMPLACENCY
EXPOSED

A Study of the Book of Malachi

LifeWay Press®
Nashville, TN

ISBN: 978-1-4300-5344-6
Item: 005784026

Subject Area: Bible Studies
Dewey Decimal Classification Number: 224.26
Subject Heading: PROPHETIC BOOKS OF THE OLD TESTAMENT/MALACHI
Printed in the United States of America

LifeWay Christian Resources
One LifeWay Plaza
Nashville, TN 37234-0175

We believe that the Bible has God for its author; salvation for its end; and
truth, without any mixture of error, for its matter and that all Scripture is totally
true and trustworthy. To review LifeWay's doctrinal guidelines, please visit
www.lifeway.com/doctrinalguideline.

Unless otherwise indicated, all Scripture quotations are from the Holman
Christian Standard Bible®, Copyright © 1999, 2000, 2002, 2003 by Holman
Bible Publishers. Holman Christian Standard Bible®, Holman CSB®, and HCSB®
are federally registered trademarks of Holman Bible Publishers.
Used by permission.

Scripture quotations marked ESV are from The Holy Bible, English Standard
Version®, copyright © 2001 by Crossway Bibles, a publishing ministry of Good
News Publishers. All rights reserved.

Scripture quotations marked NIV are taken from The Holy Bible, New
International Version®, NIV®, Copyright © 1973, 1978, 1984, 2011 by Biblica, Inc.
Used by permission. All rights reserved.

Scripture quotations marked NLT are from the Holy Bible, New Living
Translation, copyright © 1996. Used by permission of Tyndale House Publishers,
Inc., Wheaton, IL 60189 USA. All rights reserved.

Cover Image, Title Page Image, Contents Page Image, Chapter Beginnings Image,
and Learning Activities Image: IStock Photo

Contents

Complacency Exposed

Most teenagers are remarkably similar creatures. For instance, independent of each other, most implement a similar strategy when confronted with an error. It may present itself like this:

A father walks into his son's room and informs the son he will not be allowed to leave the house that evening since he had not cleaned his room as instructed. The teenager is incredulous, for in his mind he has cleaned his room and asks, with typical teenage sarcasm, what the dad means that the room is not clean.

Trying to be patient and maintain his composure, the father observes that he and his wife had explicitly told the boy to clean his room, yet there were still things everywhere. The son retorts that he has organized the room and knows where everything is.

With growing frustration, dad points out that there are still dirty clothes piled up in the corner. The son shoots back that's better than them being everywhere.

Dad barks back that he had clearly stated everything had to be off the floor, to which the son asks, "Well, what did you mean by *everything?*"

Even though conversations like this can be uncomfortable for all involved, they are needed. Parental parameters are not enforced for cruelty, but for protection, and obedience in the little things will lead to obedience in the big things.

Love can be demonstrated by a protective warning as much as by a display of affection. When a sheep is about to walk over a cliff, it is a loving act to crook its neck rather than allow it to fall. Our relationship with God is no different.

Throughout the Book of Malachi, we will see how God, as a loving Father, confronted, corrected, and challenged the people of Israel for straying from Him.

Malachi called for Israel to return to God before the Messiah arrived on earth. It is a short but theologically deep and weighty book. It contains significant material requiring careful examination.

This introduction will lay out five details about Malachi that will aid in understanding its words.

The Author of the Book

The name *Malachi* means "my messenger" or "my angel." Rightly translated, both of these are correct, for *angel* literally

Shepherd and flock
in Israel.
COREL PHOTO

means "messenger," but that causes a problem for many in the modern audience: we are forced to determine whether this is a human messenger or a heavenly one.

Throughout this book, there are four references to a messenger of the Lord:

1:1 - where it is rendered as a proper name, "The word of the LORD to Israel through Malachi";

2:7 - where it refers to any member of the priesthood, declaring "he is the messenger of the LORD of Hosts";

3:1a - meaning forerunner to the Messiah, "My messenger";

3:1b - alluding to the Messiah Himself, "the Messenger of the covenant."

It's difficult to determine exactly who Malachi was because there is no mention in the book of his father's name, nor of his place of birth. Some have therefore concluded the book is anonymous, written by some unkown-to-us messenger of God. Some people believe Malachi, "My messenger," is a title for Ezra the Scribe.

Let's narrow the search. It can be inferred that the writer was a contemporary of Nehemiah, because both of them dealt with similar time-sensitive issues, such as:

- The improper conduct of the priesthood: Nehemiah 13:1-9 and Malachi 1:6–2:9.
- The diminishing concern for tithing: Nehemiah 13:10-13 and Malachi 3:8-12.
- Intermarriage between Jews and Gentiles: Nehemiah 13:23-28 and Malachi 2:11-16.

Furthermore, because Malachi is used as a proper name instead of a title, we will operate under the premise that Malachi was a human prophet. But the text never emphasizes the writer of these words, just the message.

The Audience of the Book

Israel was the recipient of this message. By addressing the book "to Israel" (1:1) rather than "to Israel and Judah," Malachi indicated that there were no longer two separate Jewish kingdoms, a Northern Kingdom and a Southern Kingdom. This points to a time after 539-538 B.C., when Cyrus of Persia conquered Babylon and permitted foreign peoples, including the Jews, to return to the land of their fathers.

The Occasion of the Book

As will be exposed throughout this commentary, moral degradation was common, including adultery, divorce, falsehood, fraud, and sorcery running rampant throughout the people. The source of some of the corruption was the priests themselves. As already mentioned, intermarriage between Jews and unbelieving

Gentiles, a practice prohibited in the Mosaic Law, was commonplace. Additionally, traditionalism was beginning to trump the commands of Scripture, laying the foundation for both Pharisaism and Sadduceeism.

The prophecies and warnings that Malachi would deliver bear a special weight also because the book is the final prophetic work of the Old Testament before the coming of Christ. A 400-year silence from God would be broken by Gabriel's prediction of John's and Jesus' births in Luke: the direct fulfillment of the promise in Malachi that God would send a messenger. As readers who have already encountered the promised Messiah, we can view the unprecedented miracle represented here: God entered into His own story and played the key role in His own providential plan.

The Oracle of the Book

Malachi acknowledged Divine inspiration as the source of his words in order to eliminate any doubts in the minds of the hearers, as revealed in the first verse of the book. God Himself delivered the prophetic oracle, Malachi wrote it down, and then he proclaimed it to the people of Israel.

Malachi's tone was threatening to the people, as if he were saying, "I swear that this is going to happen. You can take this to the bank: God's punishment is imminent if you don't repent."

The Hebrew word *massa* is translated into English to read "oracle," but also means "burden" or "load." Traditionally, *massa* could be used as a judgment against a person, as in the case of the prophecy against Ahab in 2 Kings 9:25-26, in which the word is sometimes translated to mean "prophecy" (NIV) or "pronouncement" (ESV). In Malachi, though, *massa* signifies judgment against the nation of Israel. This pronouncement was not the word not of a man, but of God.

If this is a word straight from God, why was it a burden for Malachi to deliver it to the nation of Israel?

We must remember that the office of prophet was not something one aspired to, as one might aspire to a political position or business role. It was a calling, much like a pastor or shepherd.

The prophet had two distinct functions:

1. The function of the prophet was to call the people and the nation back to the ways of God, according to Deuteronomy 18:15-18. The covenant of the Old Testament blessed faithful obedience and disciplined disobedience.

2. The prophet sometimes would deliver predictive messages, including those about the coming Messiah.

As with a megaphone held to the mouth of an announcer, the prophet broadcast the message of God unto the people, much like the expository preacher does today when he delivers the Word from behind the pulpit. At one time, God spoke directly to Adam and Eve in the garden, and directly to Moses on Mount Sinai. But the rescued Hebrew people asked not to hear His voice directly (Ex. 20:18-19). From that time on, God primarily used prophets to be His voice and witness both with their mouths and ministries.

People who self-proclaim the title of prophet should be taken with caution, for the life of a prophet is indescribably difficult. Think of Isaiah. God instructed him to discard his outer garments and sandals, and then walk naked around the city for 3 years as a visual sign to the people of Israel of the coming captivity of Egypt and Cush, and Israel if they chose to align themselves with those nations (Isa. 20:1-4). Imagine God saying to your pastor, "Your people are stiff-necked and selfish. They are not getting the message. I want you to take off the suit and tie. In fact, take everything off and walk the halls of your church disrobed for three years as a sign of warning to the members."

The Style and Structure of the Book

The book radiates with rich theology, covering themes such as the nature and majesty of God, the coming Messiah, and the steadfast love of the Lord.

Six speeches provide a framework for Malachi's structure:

Speech 1—1:2-5	God's Love
Speech 2—1:6-2:9	Unfaithfulness of the Priests
Speech 3—2:10-16	Divorce
Speech 4—2:17-3:5	Divine Justice
Speech 5—3:6-12	Tithe
Speech 6—3:13-4:3	Day of Judgment

Malachi used the Socratic dialectic method of communication. Socrates was a classical Greek philosopher who cross-examined someone in order to uncover contradictions or inconsistencies in their assertions. Rather than teaching by coming right out and stating a conclusion, the dialectic style merely piles questions on top of each other, in order to make the conclusion come from within the student—and, thus, make the lesson stick.

The Socratic dialectic method of teaching brings answers not from the mouth of the teacher to the ears of the student, but rather from the heart of the student into his mind. Rabbis used this same approach constantly, and so did Jesus: much of His teaching was done by merely asking questions.

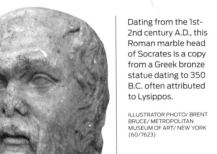

If a rebuke is raised against you, it is easy to brush it off as just a negative, misunderstanding opinion. However, should the accusation be raised in the form of a probing question, so that a realization of the error of your ways comes from within rather than from without, it is no longer a mere outside, misinformed opinion; it is an opportunity for reflection, self-examination, and repentance. But just because the method God used to do this is effective does not mean it is easy. That is what makes it such a profound expression of love.

How a person handles correction speaks volumes about their character. The author of Hebrews wrote:

> My son, do not take the Lord's discipline lightly or faint when you are reproved by Him, for the Lord disciplines the one He loves and punishes every son He receives. No discipline seems enjoyable at the time, but painful. Later on, however, it yields the fruit of peace and righteousness to those who have been trained by it (Heb. 12:5-6,11).

This is why Malachi began his book with the words, "'I have loved you,' says the LORD" (1:2).

God loves you so much that He is willing to bear the difficult burden of exposing your sin. He loves you so much that He doesn't allow you to wallow in it. Our study of the Book of Malachi will demonstrate for us just how He went about doing that several centuries before the birth of Jesus.

CHAPTER ONE

[handwritten: "Tough Love" 2-26-17]

How Have You Loved Us?

[handwritten: He has chosen us (me)]

MALACHI 1:1-5

The rocky history of Israel in the Old Testament testifies to how often God's chosen people were oblivious to His unconditional love for them. They had forgotten God's sustenance through the desert, protection from their adversaries, and punishment of their enemies. As we approach Malachi, let us begin the same way that the oracle of the Word of the Lord appeared to Malachi:

"I have loved you," says the LORD. But you ask "How have You loved us?" "Wasn't Esau Jacob's brother?" This is the LORD's declaration. "Even so, I loved Jacob, but I hated Esau. I turned his mountains into a wasteland, and gave his inheritance to the desert jackals" (Mal. 1:2-3).

Before we unpack this portion of the text, let us venture back to the covenant relationship God made with a man in the Book of Genesis (12:1-3). The passage in Malachi assumes a couple of things: it assumes readers have an understanding of God's covenant with Abraham, the portion of Scripture to which it is referring, but even more than that, it assumes the readers have a thorough knowledge of the history of the nation of Israel. Let us briefly recall this history, so we can be caught up with the historical context which Malachi addressed.

God called a man named Abram to leave his home in Ur and follow Him to another land, and Abram, by faith, obeyed. God made a covenant with him, declaring that he would be the father of many nations. God solidified that covenant by giving Abram a new name: Abraham. His new name would serve as a reminder of God's promise that his descendants would be more numerous than the stars.

Abraham fathered his first child with his servant Hagar. The second, miraculously, came through his aged wife Sarah. The miraculous birth of Isaac, the son by Sarah, was another reminder of God's promise to Abraham. Isaac was the son through whom the nation of Israelites would come. Abraham's life was filled with tests from God to reveal his unwavering commitment to Him.

Isaac had twin boys named Esau and Jacob. Esau was born first, and thus had the right to the blessing of his father, but he despised his birthright and sold it to

Jacob for a bowl of stew. Jacob would later con their father out of the blessing intended for Esau, leading to Jacob's fleeing to save his own life from an angry Esau, who perhaps waited too long to prize what was rightfully his to begin with.

Jacob proved his zeal for receiving God's favor and blessing throughout his life. One night he found himself wrestling with the Lord in a field near the Jabbok River, just outside the Jordan Valley. As a result of Jacob's striving for God's blessing, God rewarded him in much the same way that He had rewarded his grandfather, Abraham: God made a covenant with him and changed his name to Israel, which means "He strives with God."

God's promise to Abraham to be the father of nations was coming to fruition. His descendants were known as the Israelites, after the name God gave Jacob for his faithfulness. The Israelites flourished until they were later enslaved in Egypt for over four hundred years. God raised up an unlikely leader named Moses who would lead the captives out from the bondage of Pharaoh toward the promised land.

Jabbok River, outside of Amman, Jordan; After crossing the Jabbok, Jacob wrestled with the Lord.

ILLUSTRATOR PHOTO/KRISTEN HILLER (37/0035)

Despite a golden age under the rule of David, the positive political and spiritual situation of God's people quickly turned sour. After David's son Solomon died, Israel was split into two kingdoms—the Northern Kingdom (Israel) and the Southern Kingdom (Judah). Subsequently, the Assyrians took Israel into exile in 722 B.C., and Judah followed a century and a half later in 586 B.C. at the hands of Nebuchadnezzar, the ruler of the Babylonian Empire. Jerusalem was destroyed, the walls were knocked down, and the temple was burned. The history of God's covenant people had come full circle. They were again scattered and enslaved as they had been in Egypt.

Many of God's prophets predicted that this exile was temporary. Their enslavement would eventually end, allowing the people to return to the land promised by God to their forefathers. Jeremiah 29:10 prophetically states: "When 70 years for Babylon are complete, I will attend to you and will confirm My promise concerning you to restore you to this place." The return occurred in three progressions.

First, Zerubbabel led an assembly back to the land and laid the foundations for the temple. After a lengthy delay, construction was eventually completed. The last three books of the Old Testament—Haggai, Zechariah, and Malachi—were all written after this return. Second, Ezra, the scribe, spearheaded a massive movement to re-establish scriptural worship in Israel and the temple that Zerubbabel had rebuilt. Third, under the leadership of Nehemiah, the people banded together to rebuild the walls around Jerusalem.

One might think Israel would have learned its lesson, particularly after seeing the great lengths to which God had remained faithful to His covenants with them and His sustained loyalty after all of the years. Such is not the case. The people of Israel were corrupted again, this time originating with the very top of their religious leaders: the priests. The corruption of the priesthood had a trickle-down effect on the people, prompting the prophetic word that came through Malachi.

Malachi's book begins with a reminder of the beginning of the nation by referencing Jacob and Esau, which would have called to mind the rest of the story, leading up to the time of the writing. Prophets speaking God's Word often put the good news before the bad. Before extending an indictment of Israel's priestly class, Malachi reminded and reaffirmed God's sovereign love to His people.

Personal Reflection:

1. Read Genesis 25:19-26. Who were Jacob and Esau? What do we know about their relationship?

2. Some perceive the God of the Old Testament to be strict and harsh in His punishments. Read the following Old Testament passages and record what you learn about the God of love?
   - Exodus 15:1,11-13

   - Numbers 14:18-19

   - Psalm 5:7

The broad wall; This city wall was apparently built in the days of Hezekiah, king of Judah (late 8th century B.C.) as part of his refortifying the city in preparation for an Assyrian attack. The wall was built partly over the ruins of earlier houses, which were destroyed to make way for the wall (see Isa. 22:10 - "You counted the houses of Jerusalem so that you could tear them down to fortify the wall.). This wall, 7 meters thick, has been exposed for a length of 65 meters of which, 45 meters are still visible, running from north to south. The unusual thickness of the wall suggests that this might be the "Broad Wall" mentioned in Nehemiah 3:8 and 12:38.

ILLUSTRATOR PHOTO/JUSTIN VENEMAN (35/68/84)

God's Love Demonstrated
Through His Declaration

The word **loved** in Malachi 1:2 is in what we would call the present perfect tense, which implies an action that has been completed in the past, but continues having ramifications up through the present. In English, we employ this tense by saying "have loved," which means it began at some point in the past and continues true through today. The Hebrew word used here is *ahab*, which is used repeatedly in the Old Testament. It is frequently used to explain God's love for Israel. The New American Commentary describes this kind of affection:

> Terms for "love" were common in ancient Near Eastern treaties as synonyms for covenant loyalty. In Mesopotamian texts, divine love also motivated selection of a king.... Likewise in the Hebrew Bible, especially in Deuteronomy, *ahab*, "love," often is found in texts dealing with choosing and with faithfulness.[1]

God's love was the reason for choosing Israel (Deut. 7:7-8), and His good pleasure was the only reason for continuing to care for them. God first demonstrated His love for His people by reminding them of how He had redeemed their ancestors from bondage in Egypt. He brought to mind the exclusive relationship He had established with those ancestors, and His steadfast love toward them. Notice that all of this was before He gave Israel the Law. In the Old Testament, relationship always precedes requirement. As C. J. H. Wright explains, "God did not send Moses down to Egypt with the law already tucked under his cloak."[2] Instead, He miraculously delivered them from the oppression of the Egyptians, protected them from the 10 plagues, and supernaturally parted the Red Sea before giving the Law. That is, God showed grace to the generation under the guidance of Moses before making covenantal demands. Likewise, God, in Malachi 1:2, reminded the Jews of His grace before reminding them of His Law.

God's love is unconditional. We do nothing to earn it. We don't deserve it. Yet, He graciously lavishes it upon us. Man can do nothing to sway God to love us more. We can do nothing to cause Him to love us any less. No one in this world will ever love us like God the Father. John the apostle stated, "We love because He first loved us," and "God's love was revealed among us in this way: God sent His One and Only Son into the world so that we might live through Him. Love consists in this: not that we loved God, but that He loved us and sent His Son to be the propitiation for our sins." (1 John 4:9-10,19). Author Max Lucado describes God's love in this manner: "If [God] had a refrigerator, your picture would be on it."[3] All the redeemed can sing in unison of God's amazing love that caused His Son, our King, to die for us.

1. Richard A. Taylor and E. Ray Clendenen, vol. 21 A, *Haggai, Malachi*, The New American Commentary (Nashville: Broadman & Holman Publishers, 2004), 247.
2. C.J. H. Wright, "Eye for an Eye," quoted in Taylor and Clendenen, 248.
3. Max Lucado, *God Thinks You're Wonderful* (Nashville: Thomas Nelson, 2003), 13.

When you argue σ God —

God Demonstrates His Love for His People Through His Election

you'll never win,

Even though God disclosed to them how much He loved them, the nation of Israel questioned God's affection by inquiring: **"How have You loved us?"** as if God had not kept His promise to restore the tribes and the land. It appears they were only seeing their present situation and had completely forgotten how God had sustained them and demonstrated His love for them consistently throughout the years.

LEARNING ACTIVITY

How Have You Loved Me?

Questioning God's love was not unique in Malachi's day. Many Christians today are tempted to ask the same questions of God that the Israelites asked. Look at the list below and underline situations that you, or someone you know, have experienced. List other situations that you or others have experienced. Circle any experience that led you to doubt God's love.

- Loss of a loved one
- Financial difficulty
- Misconduct by a trusted leader
- Long-term illness or disability
- Loss of a job
- Wayward child
- Sexual abuse
- Marital difficulties
- Other circumstances:

(1) The Burden of His Word
A. the Source of His Authority
"word of God"
B. Speaker of His Responsibility
"by Malachi"
C. Subjects of His Identity
"to Israel"

(2) Blessing of His Love V2
A. Chosen through love
B. Changed by Love

God, understanding the people needed a history lesson, began by reminding them of how He had regarded Jacob over Esau. Malachi 1:2b-3a states, "**'Wasn't Esau Jacob's brother?' This is the L**ORD**'s declaration. 'Even so, I loved Jacob, but I hated Esau.'**"

The words **loved** and **hated** shouldn't be read the way we would read them today—they should be understood in a covenantal sense. Perhaps *chosen* and *not chosen* are more accurate ways of understanding just what these words are saying. Since God chose Jacob to fulfill the Abrahamic covenant, He "loved" him. Since God did not choose Esau, He "hated" him. Even though Jacob was not the firstborn, God went against the convention of giving priority to the firstborn son by choosing Jacob. According to the apostle Paul, this choice took place prior to the birth of the twins:

> Rebekah received a promise when she became pregnant by one man, our ancestor Isaac. For though her sons had not been born yet or done anything good or bad, so that God's purpose according to election might stand—not from works but from the One who calls—she was told: The older will serve the younger. As it is written: I have loved Jacob, but I have hated Esau. (Rom. 9:10-13)

Jesus utilized the same word in instructing His disciples on the expectations for being a disciple in Luke 14:25-26, "Now great crowds were traveling with Him. So He turned and said to them: 'If anyone comes to Me and does not **hate** his own father and mother, wife and children, brothers and sisters—yes, and even his own life—he cannot be My disciple'" (emphasis added). He was not suggesting we foster hatred toward our parents or siblings; rather, He demands full allegiance to Him. If you have a choice, He is always first, above acquaintances, friends, and even family.

God went against the standard rules regarding choosing the firstborn son by selecting Jacob. God's choice, then, is not influenced by human interaction or cooperation because He chose one of the twins before birth. He is a God of choice. He chose Abraham out of all the peoples of the world. He chose Abraham's son, Isaac, instead of his half-brother, Ishmael. He chose Jacob over his older brother, Esau. He chose the Israelites over all other nations. However, He chose none of them based on meritorious works they had done. Deuteronomy 7:7-8 states,

> The LORD was devoted to you and chose you, not because you were more numerous than all peoples, for you were the fewest of all peoples. But because the LORD loved you and kept the oath He swore to your fathers, He brought you out with a strong hand and redeemed you from the place of slavery, from the power of Pharaoh king of Egypt.

Paul spoke repeatedly of God's choosing throughout his epistles. In the Book of Romans, he stated, "In the same way, then, there is also at the present time a remnant chosen by grace. Now if by grace, then it is not by works; otherwise grace ceases to be grace. What then? Israel did not find what it was looking for, but the elect did find it. The rest were hardened" (Rom. 11:5-7). In his letter to the church at Ephesus, Paul wrote, "For He chose us in Him, before the foundation of the world, to be holy and blameless in His sight" (Eph. 1:4). When Paul wrote to Titus, he said, "But when the kindness of God our Savior and His love for mankind appeared, He saved us—not by works of righteousness that we had done, but according to His mercy, through the washing of regeneration and renewal by the Holy Spirit" (Titus 3:4-5).

Paul believed in God's election. He even provided a commentary on Malachi 1 in Romans 9:

> Rebekah received a promise when she became pregnant by one man, our ancestor Isaac. For though her sons had not been born yet or done anything good or bad, so that God's purpose according to election might stand—not from works but from the One who calls—she was told: The older will serve the younger. As it is written: I have loved Jacob, but I have hated Esau. (Rom. 9:10-13)

Election is not a word to shy away from. It's a biblical truth that should be understood theologically.

The point of Malachi 1:2-3 is that God does not grade on a curve. If He did, Esau might have passed with flying colors, and Jacob might have failed miserably, since he won his birthright by manipulating his older brother and his father. According to this reasoning, Esau deserved God's blessing. Yet God does not bestow grace on those who "deserve" it, for no one does. If one's righteousness were the condition for God's grace, not one person would enter the kingdom. All would experience separation from Him in a Christless place called hell if salvation were based on human achievement of righteousness. But that is what is so amazing about grace! The point is not that God loved Jacob more than Esau, but that He desired to make a covenant with Jacob instead of Esau, so that He may be brought the utmost glory. The reason that the prophet brings in the concept of God's choice in Malachi 1 is not to create a sense of exclusion, but rather to remind the people of God that their faith was not unfounded—they had been chosen, and God remained faithful to His choice to love them.

God's electing love is not based on performance, position, or power. It's based on His prerogative. The input one has in being chosen is the same input one has in choosing one's parents, the country in which one is born, or the city in which one was raised. In the same way, the Jewish audience of Malachi had done nothing to deserve God's grace and love. But they received it nonetheless, and were reminded of it.

Personal Reflection:

1. As a parent, how would you respond if your child asked, "How have you loved me?"

2. What evidence of God's love and grace can you point to in your life?

3. What does it mean to be chosen by God? Why is this significant in affirming His love for us?

4. What life situations might lead someone to conclude God doesn't love him/her?

God Demonstrates His Love for His People Through His Rejection

Quite prominent in this passage is God's rejection of Edom, the descendants of Esau, which is a response to their wickedness. Notice in the text that there is a contrast between wicked Edom and blessed Israel. Since the Edomites demonstrated pride, arrogance, and violence, Malachi declared that God is righteous in His harsh punishment of that nation. In this punishment, Edom would experience two closely connected penalties for their unrighteousness: 1) The land would be destroyed and left completely uninhabited by humans; 2) The land would be possessed by the demonic (i.e., **cursed**).[4] The Edomites, as both Scripture declares and history proves, were bent toward destruction. One commentator expresses it this way:

> Esau's descendants would be excluded *as a nation* from that special electing love that would belong to Israel. God's choosing Jacob and his descendants meant that He established a permanent relationship with Israel as a whole, in which He would instruct them with truth, train them with righteousness, care for them with compassion, bless them with goodness, and discipline them with severity; regardless of how often they strayed from Him, He would be faithful to them by His grace until His work in them was complete and "all Israel" (Rom. 11:26, referring back to true Israel in Rom. 9:6) would enjoy the righteousness, peace, and joy that come from knowing God (Jer. 33; Ezek. 36; Acts 13:16-41; Rom. 9–11).[5]

Malachi's prophecy came to fruition in 550 B.C. when the Nabataean Arabs forced the Edomites to settle in Idumea, which is just south of Judea (where the Israelites lived). Because of the hatred between these two groups of people, tensions would continue between the people of Jacob/Israel and the people of Esau/Edom. In 37 B.C., Herod the Great, an Idumean, began to rule in Judea as a client-ruler of the Roman Empire.

When Rome was at the height of its power, it would appoint state-approved rulers to govern the places they had conquered, so they could exercise control over what was, at the time, the entire known world. They appointed this Edomite Herod over the land, perhaps recognizing the ancestral relationship between Idumea and Israel and figuring that

4. Micah Fries, Stephen Rummage, and Robby Gallaty, *Christ-Centered Exposition Commentary: Exalting Jesus in Zephaniah, Haggai, Zechariah, Malachi* (Nashville:B&H Publishing Group, 2015), 209.
5. Taylor and Clendenen, 253.

he, having this connection with them, would rule them fairly and appropriately for their culture. Unfortunately, though, they did not understand the situation fully. As a result, the story of Jacob and Esau was again played out in the interaction between Jesus and Herod, in a connection that is staggering. Herod, this Roman appointee, was worried when he heard of the one "born King of the Jews" (Matt. 2:2). Like Jacob, Jesus was appointed by God. Like Esau, Herod was not!

God's love for Israel should not be left to speculation. He pointed the people to a historical event to prove His love: the people of God had been brought back from Babylonian captivity while the land of Edom remained in perpetual ruin.

Personal Reflection:

1. Read Hebrews 12:3-11. How do you explain the relationship between love and discipline?

2. Reflect on how you approach worship. How does the reality of God's choosing to show you grace instead of justice impact the way you worship?

Christ as the Pinnacle Display of God's Love

Let us bring this first passage into the modern day for a moment. Reading about the suffering and destruction of God's people, you may question: "How do I know God loves me?" The answer to this question, like in Malachi's day, is found in a historical event, the cross of Jesus Christ. Romans 5:8 declares, "God proves His own love for us." How? "In that while we were still sinners, Christ died for us!" The cross stands as a historical landmark to the bold declaration with which Malachi opened his prophecy: God loves us. Jesus Christ is the pinnacle display of God's sovereign love.

As He did with Israel, God chooses to love us, which places the initiative upon God. The Scripture says we were once wayward in sin unable to save ourselves. We were alienated from God (Col. 1:21), dead in our trespasses and sins (Eph. 2:1-2),

The fourteenth station of the cross on the Via Dolorosa is in the Church of the Holy Sepulcher. It was here that Jesus is believed to have been laid in the tomb.

blinded by the enemy (2 Cor. 4:3), morally bankrupt (Gen. 8:21), and defiled in our bodies (Rom. 1:24-25). Yet God saw our condition and initiated our adoption. Ephesians 1:3-6 states:

> Praise the God and Father of our Lord Jesus Christ, who has blessed us in Christ with every spiritual blessing in the heavens. For He chose us in Him, before the foundation of the world, to be holy and blameless in His sight. In love He predestined us to be adopted through Jesus Christ for Himself, according to His favor and will, to the praise of His glorious grace that He favored us with in the Beloved.

God's initiative, then, is a biblical expression of His love for us in Christ. His choice of us is meant to humble us, remove boasting, remove entitlement, remove pride, and eradicate self-reliance. It should lead us to worship, realizing none of us deserves heaven. Yet, God in His kindness extended grace to us at the moment of our salvation.   *P+L*

God's love is unconditional. The nation of Israel did nothing to deserve being chosen by Him or being delivered from slavery, and, in the same way, you did nothing to deserve His love. Even when we stray, He runs to meet us, just as the loving father did in the parable of the prodigal son (see Luke 15). The father of the wayward son, who represents God in the story, ran to embrace his repentant son, even though the son asked for his inheritance early (which was tantamount to telling his father, "Hurry up and die already!") and had squandered it! There was no way the son could pay his father back, nor did the father wish him to! He wanted nothing but reciprocal love from his son, and this is all God wants from us. We can do nothing good to persuade Him to love us more. Neither can we do anything wrong to make Him love us any less. No one will ever love you like God loves you (see 1 John 4:9,19) and the only proper response is to love Him back.

amen

Personal Reflection:
1. How does Malachi 1:1-5 communicate hope?

2. How can the realization that God loves you affect a hopeless situation in your life? How will it affect your worship?

Beyond the Borders

Malachi 1:5 declares the people would one day realize "The LORD is great, even beyond the borders of Israel." One of the reasons God has chosen to save us is so His glory can be declared beyond our borders. These may be geographical borders, but they may also be cultural, social, economic, or language borders. List places or people that you would consider to be beyond your borders.

Circle one item from your list that you would covenant to pray for. Ask God to help you to be willing to go beyond your borders and reach out into that area/group of people.

3-12-17

CHAPTER TWO

How Have We Despised Your Name?

MALACHI 1:6–2:9

I t is an unfortunate reality that words like *excellent, devoted,* and *committed* are almost exclusively used in our culture to describe the work ethic of athletes, career men and women, and those who take pride in their hobbies or pastimes. Unfortunately, these same descriptors are often absent from our lips in describing the whole-hearted devotion of our brothers and sisters in the Lord. Indeed, if we are honest, we know that we, too, lack such devotion in our own worship and obedience.

The same lack of devotion was present in Israel during the time Malachi wrote. God had given His people the best. He had redeemed them from the Egyptians, led them through the desert, revealed the land to them, extended to them the basic necessities of life for herdsmen, marched them into the promised land, and conquered their enemies. But what was their response to His steadfast love for them? While one would think it would be extravagant praise and loving obedience, the people instead offered Him what can only be described as worthless worship.

As we examine this text, we would do well to examine the current state of our own worship and attitude toward the Lord to determine if it is meaningful—worthy of the God who has saved us in His Son Jesus Christ—or worthless.

First it may be helpful to ask what is meant by the term *worship.* Most Christians, when they think of worship, immediately imagine singing, praying, or a certain posture. To be sure, worship might include all of these aspects, but it must also be more than these. Worship is an attitude of one's heart. It's from the old word that means "worthship." It's to ascribe to an individual or thing honor and respect. It is to proclaim the worth of the object.

In Israel's case (as in ours), we must examine our devotion to God. We worship God most importantly because of who He is: the supreme Creator and Ruler of the universe. But we also worship Him for what He has done for us. Examine for a moment Malachi 1:6:

> "A son honors his father, and a servant his master. But if I am a father, where is My honor? And if I am a master, where is your fear of Me? says Yahweh of Hosts to you priests, who despise My name." Yet you ask: "How have we despised Your name?"

The word *hosts* is a military term referring to an army. In this instance, it is a reference to the army of **Yahweh,** likely the angels. Hence, Malachi reminded the reader that God deserves respect not only like a **father** of a household or **master** of a house; God demands honor based on His status as the divine general (or perhaps "commander-in-chief," using modern political terms) of the angelic armies.

So it is clear that Israel's God called for proper worship of who He is and what He had done for them. Because He had set His love upon Israel like a father upon a child, and because He is the master of an army of angels, He is worthy of meaningful worship. Already in verse 6 we see that God was not receiving the worship due His name, and He held the **priests,** in particular, responsible for this failure.

Personal Reflection:

1. Who do you admire for their devotion? What would your worship of God look like if it reflected such devotion?

2. How does our worship reveal how highly we esteem God's name?

Israel's Priests Practiced Depraved Worship (Mal. 1:6-12)

"A son honors his father, and a servant his master. But if I am a father, where is My honor? And if I am a master, where is your fear of Me? says Yahweh of Hosts to you priests, who despise My name." Yet you ask: "How have we despised Your name?" (v. 6)

God is referred to in this passage and all throughout Scripture as a **father.** He was the father of Israel. Why? Because He created and redeemed them. Like a loving father, He nurtured them. Like a loving father, He disciplined them when they were disobedient. God said in the Ten Commandments, "Honor your father and your mother." Is it any wonder, then, that God expects obedience as a spiritual father?

However, we see in the text that Israel did not obey Him as a child obeys a father. In the first place, they offered Him no honor. That word **honor** is an interesting word. It's the Hebrew word *kabod,* which is elsewhere translated "glory." They did not glory in Him. They did not revere Him. They did not respect Him.

Then the Lord issued a second indictment: Israel did not **fear** God. We must be careful not to take this word *fear* only in the sense of being scared or frightened. This word also denotes an appropriate respect, a reverential honor for holy God. What God is saying through the prophet Malachi is, "You have not honored Me, and you do not respect Me."

The text clearly places the blame for that upon the **priests.** These had ceased to be Israel's spiritual examples. God expected them to be ministerial servants in the temple, commissioned to carry out sacrifices and lead the festivals and feasts. The depth of their failure is seen in that, despite their privileged position, they **despised** God.

The term *despise* is significant. It is the attitude of ongoing disrespect. It also refers to the act of conveying insignificance or worthlessness upon an object, idea, or individual. It is the same word used in the Genesis 25:34 concerning Esau and Jacob, when Esau considered his birthright insignificant, so much so that he could trade it away for stewed meat. In the present context, the priests are said to despise God's name, which is shorthand for His person, character, and work. They despised who God was. He wasn't important to them anymore. He wasn't striking to them anymore. He wasn't significant to them anymore. Even though they offered sacrifices, they considered God to be without worth, and this misinterpretation affected the form of their worship.

Personal Reflection:

1. How had God shown Himself to be a father to the people of Israel? How had God shown Himself to be a father to you?

2. What are some contemporary characteristics of worthless worship?

Israel's Priests Despised God's Name in Their Contribution

At the end of verse 6, Malachi gave a voice to the thoughts of the priests. God knew their hearts and revealed to them how they had despised His name:

> "By presenting defiled food on My altar." You ask: "How have we defiled You?" When you say: "The LORD's table is contemptible." (Mal. 1:7)

The priests asked, "God, how in the world is offering unclean sacrifices defiling you? How is our offering contaminating, Lord?" To this God responded, "Just look at what you've done!"

What they were doing was no minor sin. **Defiled** can also be translated *unclean* or *polluted*. This is a ritual way of saying unauthorized or unacceptable. God viewed the sacrifices very seriously. When Aaron's two sons, Nadab and Abihu, offered unauthorized sacrifices to the Lord, do you remember what the Lord did (see Lev. 10:1-3)? He sent down fire and consumed them! But in spite of such a stark example of the holiness God demands, the priests here were offering unclean sacrifices to the Lord and acting as if nothing were wrong. Examine verse 8:

> "When you present a blind animal for sacrifice, is it not wrong? And when you present a lame or sick animal, is it not wrong? Bring it to your governor! Would he be pleased with you or show you favor?" asks the LORD of Hosts.

Limestone four horned altar from Megiddo; dating from 975-925 B.C. Sacrificial altars with four corner horns have been found throughout the southern Levant and are described in numerous places in the Bible. This example from Megiddo is too small to have been used for animal sacrifices, and was likely used for the sacrifice of grains, wine, or incense.

ILLUSTRATOR PHOTO/G.B. HOWELL/ ORIENTAL INSTITUTE MUSEUM OF CHICAGO (67/5763)

Malachi pointed out that the priests were offering crippled, lame, or blinded animals to the Lord, even though God expected a spotless sacrifice. He didn't want second best. He didn't want third best. He wanted the very best they had.

By God asking this question, the answer should have been obvious: **"Is it not wrong?"** Absolutely it was! It was embarrassing that God would even have to point this out to the priests. God was saying, "Use common sense here, guys. Don't you see how wrong this is? You should never offer this to Me, and you sure wouldn't offer this to the governor!"

When Malachi said, **"Bring it to your governor!"** he used an image people would recognize to describe this pagan leader. One commentator says,

> The governor's "table" was a lavishly prepared banquet … including "offerings" from the people. Certainly the governor … would not have been pleased with the meat of blind, crippled, or diseased animals; in fact, he would not have accepted it. How much more absurd it was to expect the favor of the Lord Almighty … with such offerings. He did not accept such sacrifices, nor did He accept the priests.[1]

In modern times, God might have reason to say something to you like this: "You offer your best to Uncle Sam, but you offer less to the work of God. You spend all your time watching college football, but you spend minimal time reading My Word. You invest all your time in your hobbies, but you devote little time to praying, seeking, memorizing, and meditating. And now you request the favor of God?" This is exactly what He said in verse 9: **"'And now ask for God's favor. Will He be gracious to us? Since this has come from your hands, will He show any of you favor?' asks the LORD of Hosts."**

The word translated *ask* means "to soften the face" or "stroke the face." In the vernacular of today, I interpret it as "buttering someone up." And as ridiculous as this sounds, we do the very same today: "God, I know I haven't come to church in a while; I know I haven't been really faithful to read the Word; I know I haven't given anything to the ministry; I know I haven't given any time to the work of sharing the gospel; I know I haven't memorized and meditated; I know I really just haven't been faithful, God, but would you PLEASE bless this situation at this time?" Of course this is not to suggest we ever earn God's blessing by actually doing any of these things, but the inconsistency is appalling! Really?! Now we want to honor God and ask Him to honor us? We betray our lack of reverence, and we despise His name with such requests.

From this rebuke we can clearly see this important truth: Before God ever accepts our gifts, He inspects our hearts. The value of the offering is determined by the heart of the one submitting it. Before we give anything to God, we must give Him ourselves completely.

---

1. J. Ronald Blue, "James," in *The Bible Knowledge Commentary: An Exposition of the Scriptures*, eds. J. F. Walvoord and R. B. Zuck, vol. 2 (Wheaton, IL: Victor Books, 1985), 1578.

This truth reminds me of the young believer who had attended church shortly after being baptized in Africa. She realized that during part of the service, they were passing an offering plate. Because she was a new believer, this was new to her. She saw people taking money out of their pockets and their wallets and putting it into the offering plate. She, as a new believer and living on menial conditions, reached into her pockets and realized she had no money. As the plate was being passed down to her row, the usher handed the plate to her. She didn't know what to do so she placed the plate on the ground and she stood inside the plate and she said out loud, "God, I don't have money but you can have all of me." Surely this was an acceptable act of worship.

The people of Israel had despised God's name. They had forgotten about His wondrous nature and His glorious works. He wasn't impressive to them anymore. Therefore, they despised and dishonored Him in their contributions. They defiled His altar, but their trespasses extend even further.

Personal Reflection:

1. How might people today reflect Israel's hypocrisy of verse 9?

2. What/who tries to claim your highest worship, which really belongs only to God?

Defiled Offerings

God described in precise detail why the blind, lame, sick, and stolen offerings that were being brought to Him were unacceptable. But do we also bring God unacceptable offerings? Beside each of the defective offerings, write one or more ways Christians today make our worship unacceptable to God. (Remember, our worship is more than what we bring to God on Sundays at church; it includes our private worship, family worship, times of spontaneous worship throughout the day, and our worship through acts of service.)

Blind—

Lame—

Sick—

Stolen—

Israel's Priests Despised God's Name in Their Commitment

Notice, also, that the people disgraced God's table:

> "I wish one of you would shut the temple doors, so you would no lon-ger kindle a useless fire on My altar! I am not pleased with you," says the LORD of Hosts, "and I will accept no offering from your hands. For My name will be great among the nations, from the rising of the sun to its setting. Incense and pure offerings will be presented in My name in every place because My name will be great among the nations," says Yahweh of Hosts. (Mal. 1:10-11)

In emphasizing how great His name will be among the nations, God was indict-ing Israel for its lack of esteem for His name. In essence, the Lord said, "Apparently My name is no longer great to you, Israel, but it will be great among the nations."

He continued to focus on their lack of commitment in verse 12: **"But you are profaning it when you say: 'The Lord's table is defiled, and its product, its food, is contemptible.'"** Their service to the Lord was monotonous. It was a job to them. The priests were merely going through the motions in the temple, and God wanted to shut them off from His presence because of it. He was sick and tired of their heartless rituals and routines. He wanted no more of their prayers and hymns. He was done with their sacrifices and feasts. His desire was for heartfelt devotion, which, judging by their commitment to His worship, was absent.

Because of their actions, God would not accept their offerings. We know the full realization of this warning took place in A.D. 70 when the temple was utterly destroyed and not one stone was left upon another. It is very difficult for modern Christians to comprehend the force of this event in Israel's history. It would be roughly similar to God saying, "Shut the doors to every church in the world. No more church. No more meetings. It's over." But that analogy doesn't really convey the whole picture, because the Israelites were dependent upon the temple for everything. They were dependent upon the temple for their sacrifices. They were dependent upon the temple for the forgiveness of their sins. They were dependent upon the temple for their festivals, for their feast days, for their offerings. The temple was even the center of national banking and Jewish political power. Without the temple, they thought the nation would cease to function.

Why would God call for such destruction? In the New Testament, we find that the temple is no longer needed because Christ is the fulfillment of everything the temple did in the life of Israel. But in Malachi 1, the reason is that the priests, the socio-religious leaders of Israel, were playing games with God. And when the leaders play games with God, it trickles down to the people. Additionally, God desires for His people to stop playing games.

We should resolve today, once and for all, that we will cease simply going through the motions. Let's be through with casual Christianity. Let's be through with worthless worship. Let's be through with selfish service that we give in order to get, and let's come before the One who knows all. We can't hide from this God. You can fool your husband. You can fool your wife. You can fool your kids. You can fool your co-workers. You can fool your Bible study group. You can fool your pastor. But you cannot fool God. In our offerings of worship and our commitment to obedience, may we give to the God of Israel meaningful, heartfelt worship.

Personal Reflection:

1. What are we called to contribute in worship? How can we despise God in our contribution?

2. How can cultural, casual Christianity resemble Israel's defective worship?

Israel's Priests Demonstrated
Apathetic Attitudes Toward Worship

Malachi proves that at the root of despondent actions are apathetic attitudes. We have viewed the priests' actions. Now let's examine their attitude:

> You also say: "Look, what a nuisance!" "And you scorn it," says the LORD of Hosts. "You bring stolen, lame, or sick animals. You bring this as an offering! Am I to accept that from your hands?" asks the LORD. "The deceiver is cursed who has an acceptable male in his flock and makes a vow but sacrifices a defective animal to the Lord. For I am a great King," says Yahweh of Hosts, "and My name will be feared among the nations." (Mal. 1:13-14)

The priests had become tired of the sacrificial system. It was a burden to them. That word **nuisance** describes a toil, a weariness, or a hardship. The priests were just burdened by the process. They had viewed their service as a system of checking boxes or punching cards and they just wanted to get their work done in order to return home to relax.

Up to this point, we've seen three categories of unacceptable sacrifice. They were offering blind, lame, and sick animals (1:8), but now God introduced a fourth category: **stolen** animals. The people weren't paying for them. These weren't the best animals they owned. They were taking them in a clandestine manner and offering them up secretly. It didn't cost them anything. And, because it cost them nothing, it was no sacrifice at all. In fact, we might say that if there's no sacrifice in your sacrifice, it's not a sacrifice.

The same applies to worship which is more than words. It's an attitude of the heart. I believe someone's offering and actions are connected to their attitude, and, in particular, to their view of God. For when we see God for who He is and what He's done, we will be deterred from playing games with Him anymore.

Nicholas Hutchinson relates the story of an archbishop of Paris about three young men traveling around Paris indulging in the sensual appetites the city offered. They sampled all the delicacies of sin, if you will, and at the end of their night, parading and perusing through the city, they found themselves on the steps of the cathedral, laid out in a drunken stupor. As they lay there, they relived their entire escapade from the night before.

One of the men had the bright idea—go inside, find a confessional booth, and confess their sins. They were going to do this in a blasphemous way, not because they wanted to be forgiven, but as the crowning glory of a night to remember. Invigorated by their laughter and intoxication, they walked into the chapel, found the priest and commenced their plan. The third young man sat in the confessional booth and began to confess his sins loudly one after the other in lurid detail.

The priest, realizing what was happening, interrupted him and said to him, "Young man, I have heard enough. You don't need to confess anything else to me. If you would like to be forgiven of your sins, you only need to do one thing. Outside of the confessional are steps leading up to an altar. On the altar is a statue of Jesus on the cross. Simply go to the statue, kneel down at the steps, look at Christ on the cross, and say these words three times, 'Lord Jesus, I know all that You've done for me and I don't care!'" The boy, as you can imagine, was shocked.

So the priest repeated those words again to him. "You will be forgiven if you go outside, look at the cross, and say to the Lord Jesus, 'I know all that You've done for me and I don't care!'" At this point, the boy stumbled out of the confessional. His friends, trying to figure out what the priest had said since they couldn't hear, watched their friend walk over to the steps. He knelt down on the stairs, looked up to Jesus hanging on the cross, and said the words with a laugh. He voiced the words a second time. But the third time, the reality of the statement stung his heart and he gave way to sincere confession and repentance. This archbishop said he knew the story to be true because it was his own.[2]

As long as the boy was playing games, his sacrifice and his worship meant nothing. When he was forced to look seriously at the God he was worshiping, he could no longer play around. The same goes for us, too.

Personal Reflection:

How do these verses help us understand God's expectation for our worship? See Romans 12:1 and 2 Corinthians 9:6-8.

God's Curse Against Israel's Priests
for Their Depraved and Apathetic Worship

"Therefore, this decree is for you priests: If you don't listen, and if you don't take it to heart to honor My name," says Yahweh of Hosts, "I will send a curse among you, and I will curse your blessings. In fact, I have already begun to curse them because you are not taking it to heart. Look, I am going to rebuke your descendants, and I will spread animal waste over your faces, the waste from your festival sacrifices, and you will be taken away with it." (Mal. 2:1-3)

God's dissatisfaction is immediately apparent in this text. In His confrontation with the priesthood, He said, "If you do not take heed the instructions, that I offered to you in Chapter 1, then you will suffer the curses detailed in Chapter 2."

The word **curse** contains a definite article in Hebrew (literally, "the curse"). This is not a casual curse nor is it a commonplace one; it is intentional and particular. Perhaps it is "the curse" from Deuteronomy 28, in which God essentially warned the people, "If you don't obey Me and you are disobedient, I will exchange blessings for destruction." Regardless of whether or not this is the specific curse God was referring to, what is certain is that "the curse" would swiftly befall the nation.

So what would be the price paid for disobedience? The punishment was twofold. First, the descendants of the Levitical priesthood will be made to suffer. Look

---

2. Nicholas Hutchinson, *Praying Each Day of the Year* (Chelmsford, Essex, United Kingdom: Matthew James Publishing Ltd., 1998) 107.

at Malachi 2:3: "Look, I am going to rebuke your descendants." This is one of six uses of the Hebrew word, here translated **Look,** in the Book of Malachi (see Mal 1:13; 2:3; 3:1 [2x]; 4:1,5). It is a word used to place emphasis upon a subject or to allude to imminence. God was emphatically telling the priesthood that He was serious. Their offspring would suffer the consequences of the current generation's actions, and they would only have themselves to blame as covenant transgressors.

Not only would the priests' offspring face judgment, but secondly, the priests themselves would be humiliated by the Lord: **"I will spread animal waste over your faces, the waste from your festival sacrifices, and you will be taken away with it"** (Mal 2:3). God certainly explained how He really felt about the disobedience of the priesthood! God's response showed the priests how repulsive He found their glib handling of His commands. By rubbing feces on their faces, He would make their outsides reflect both their insides and their sacrifices. They would be made into embarrassments, wearing their impurities for all to see.

Levi: The Role Model

In order to show the priests what they should have been doing, God then reminded them of their covenantal role model—Levi:

> "Then you will know that I sent you this decree so My covenant with Levi may continue," says the LORD of Hosts. "My covenant with him was one of life and peace, and I gave these to him; it called for reverence, and he revered Me and stood in awe of My name. True instruction was in his mouth, and nothing wrong was found on his lips. He walked with Me in peace and fairness and turned many from sin. For the lips of a priest should guard knowledge, and people should seek instruction from his mouth, because he is the messenger of the LORD of Hosts." (Mal. 2:4-7)

Levi was a man of godly commitment, character, and communication. In regards to his commitment, he is the one with whom the Lord made a covenant, and whose descendants became the Levites—the priests in God's temple. They settled disputes with judicious wisdom and served the people with humility and patience, all after Levi's example.

In regards to his character, Malachi described him using words like **reverence** or "fear," which can be taken to mean "shattered" or "dismayed." The idea is of something broken into pieces, whether physically, emotionally or spiritually. Taken with **awe,** these words together speak of great respect and reverence for holy God.

Finally, we see that Levi had direct communication with God. The true servant of God proclaims the Scripture of God. He does not alter the message to please the people. He does not shy back from doctrinal truth or speak one-sided messages to tickle the ears of people and draw big crowds. He is a man who stands on the Word of God, communicates the whole counsel of God, and leaves the results to God. The word translated **instruction** is the Hebrew word *Tora* or *Torah*, the title given to the first five books of the Old Testament. Levi had the Torah on his lips, therefore what he said was found to be without fault.

Failure to Follow Levi's Example

"You, on the other hand, have turned from the way. You have caused many to stumble by your instruction. You have violated the covenant

LEARNING ACTIVITY

Blessing or Curse?

As you consider the qualities of Levi listed in verses 5-6, write them in the left column. Then, as you review the failings of the priests in Malachi's day (vv. 8-9), list those in the right column.

Levi	Priests

of Levi," says the LORD of Hosts. "So I in turn have made you despised and humiliated before all the people because you are not keeping My ways but are showing partiality in your instruction." (Mal. 2:8-9)

We see that the priests failed on four fronts: they disobeyed the Lord, they distracted the people, they disregarded the covenant of God, and they demonstrated partiality in their instruction. As soon as the preaching of the Word was abandoned, the rest followed. They turned from the instruction of the Torah, focusing their attention where it was not supposed to be. Their judgment became impaired and skewed toward fickle human emotion.

Personal Reflection:

1. List others who have led people away from God's Word. What did they teach? How did they live?

2. Why are leaders judged more strictly?

Conclusion: Christ as the Image of God, Worthy of Spiritual Worship

Leaders are held to a higher standard than those being led. I believe every one of us repeatedly commits high treason against the Lord through our disrespect in our actions and attitudes. If we really think about our lives, we, like the priests, have wandered in our character, commitment, and communication to the Lord. Instead of being vehicles of consecration, we have become facilitators of contamination. When we get a glimpse of the greatness of God, when we get the proper perspective on who Christ is and what Christ has done for us, we'll never again play games with God.

When we see Christ as the image of God, clearly presented to us as worthy of worship and praise, we must respond with loving worship and heartfelt obedience. And, because of Christ, we are able to offer these sacrifices from a pure heart. Paul said as much in Romans 12:1: "Therefore, brothers, by the mercies of God, I urge you to present your bodies as a living sacrifice, holy and pleasing to God; this is your spiritual worship."

While Malachi was writing about Aaronic priests, a class that does not exist today, Paul said that every believer in Christ is a priest, called to offer spiritual sacrifices of worship. You don't need an outfit. You don't need a white collar. You don't need a black robe. First Peter 2:5 confirms this: "You yourselves, as living stones, are being built into a spiritual house for a holy priesthood to offer spiritual sacrifices acceptable to God through Jesus Christ." So, you and I, as priests, offer up sacrifices to the Lord.

Now what do we offer up? Let me briefly list five things. First, we offer up our bodies (see Rom. 12:1-2). Second we offer up our finances to the Lord as a spiritual sacrifice (see Phil. 4:14-18). Third, we offer up our praise to the Lord (see Heb. 13:15). Fourth, we offer up our good works (see Heb. 13:16). Finally, we even offer up those whom we have led or shared the gospel with as a witness to God (see Rom. 15:16). By God's grace, may we offer meaningful worship to the only One who is worthy of all honor and glory and praise, even among all the nations (see Mal. 1:11).

Personal Reflection:

1. How does the coming of Christ empower meaningful worship greater than was possible in the Old Testament?

2. Read Deuteronomy 28:15-68. How does this text resemble Malachi's message?

3. What does it mean to be a man or woman of godly commitment like Levi, and how do we see this perfectly manifest in Jesus?

CHAPTER THREE

Why Are We Unfaithful to One Another?

MALACHI 2:10-16

To the man who does this, may the LORD cut off any descendants from the tents of Jacob, even if they present an offering to the LORD of Hosts. And this is another thing you do: you cover the LORD's altar with tears, with weeping and groaning, because He no longer respects your offerings or receives them gladly from your hands. Yet you ask, "For what reason?" Because the LORD has been a witness between you and the wife of your youth. You have acted treacherously against her, though she was your marriage partner and your wife by covenant. Didn't the one God make us with a remnant of His life-breath? And what does the One seek? A godly offspring. So watch yourselves carefully, and do not act treacherously against the wife of your youth. "If he hates and divorces his wife," says the LORD God of Israel, "he covers his garment with injustice," says the LORD of Hosts. Therefore, watch yourselves carefully, and do not act treacherously. (Mal. 2:12-16)

One of the main contributors to the fall of Rome was the pressure of forces from within its borders. Rome's entire infrastructure crumbled because the Romans built their city and their economy on slave labor, which was unsustainable in the long run. It buckled under the weight of its gigantic ego. It allowed governmental corruption and political instability to go unchecked for too long so that its core was rotten. It forsook religion and morality for sensuous pleasures. It was the heart—the leadership—of Rome that was rotten, and that caused the rest of it to be as well.

A major point of interest in the decline and fall of Rome is that it paralleled its views on the family unit. Around the beginning of the first century A.D., the

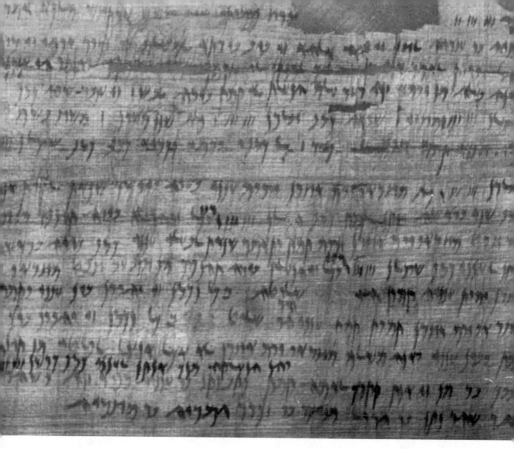

requirements for divorce were whittled down to, essentially, any reason one wanted to give. I am not saying it was only the practice of divorce that caused an entire empire to crumble, but there is a striking parallel between a nation whose people see no need to stay together in marriage when things get rough, and a nation that takes the exact same approach in the midst of national challenges.

In Malachi 2:10-16, God chastised the Israelites, particularly the priests, for the faithlessness shown to their spouses. Modern Christians are encouraged through this passage to remain faithful both to our spouses and to our first love, the Triune God.

Israel's Faithlessness to One Another

By this point in Israel's history, the tribes, though they might have been in one general geographical location, were not behaving as a people unified under the same God. Malachi asked that the out-of-sync groups renew their commitment to the Lord, and thus fix the strife between them. The first step was obviously to recognize that they shared a common Father: **"Don't all of us have one Father? Didn't one God create us? Why then do we act treacherously against one another, profaning the covenant of our fathers?"** (v. 10).

Some theologians suggest that the **one Father** is Abraham. However, this view seems to be a bit limited. More appropriately, "one Father" is most likely referring to God the Father. Look at the second part of that verse: **"Didn't one God create us?"** The word *create* is the key. It is the same word used in Genesis 1 of God creating the heavens and the earth. God was the One who formed us, and afterward chose us. It's the same idea that God tried to get through to the people in Malachi 1 when He said, "I loved Jacob, but I hated Esau."

Malachi began to assert the notion of God's choosing and calling His people—the ultimate unifying factor between them. "The only reason you people are a nation, in fact the only reason you people exist is because of Me," the Lord seemed to say. Every time that the Hebrew word is translated "create" or some variation in the Old Testament, 45 times to be exact, it is used in the context of God's sovereignty and authority.

Malachi's message was simple: "Don't forget where you came from and don't forget Who called you, because if it weren't for the sovereign call of God, where would you be?" Here's a point to ponder: forgetfulness will lead to faithlessness—the same faithlessness seen in verse 10. God rebuked their ill-treatment toward other persons in the community of faith. The phrase **one another** could be translated "our brothers" and it's this idea of the community of faith together, the tribe or the nation of Israel.

The uniform or badge that testifies to your belief in God is unity with other believers. Particularly in the Old Testament, this community of faith was the nation of Israel. In the New Testament, it is the church. The marker that proves you're a believer in the Lord Jesus Christ is your love for others, particularly the community of faith—regardless of race, nationality, or ethnicity.

Consider this logic: if it is by love that people know that we are God's, what does it mean if we do not love? Put another way: would someone be able to say of a disciple of Christ, "He's angry with everybody, he's critical of everything, or he's prejudiced against everyone around him"? The exact point that Malachi was making here is represented by the idea that the children of God must be cohesive through their love for each another. Faithlessness by the people of God toward each other suggests that they don't truly belong to the people bound by God's covenant.

Papyrus document recording the marriage of Ananiah ben Azariah and the handmaiden Tamut. Found at Elephantine. Elephantine (Yeb in Aramaic), "the city of Ivories," was situated at the southern end of a small island in the Nile. When the Persians ruled Egypt, beginning in 525 B.C., a large camp of mercenaries, including Jewish regiments, settled there. The papyrus was written in Aramaic, official language of the Persian empire.

ILLUSTRATOR PHOTO/ DAVID ROGERS/ JEWISH MUSEUM, N.Y.C. (358/6)

Personal Reflection:

1. Recall the story of how the Lord saved you. How do you see His "creating" work in your heart and life (see Mal. 2:10; Eph. 2:1-10)?

2. Compare Malachi 2:10 with Jesus' words in John 13:31-35. How are they similar? How are they different?

Israel's Faithlessness to the Precepts of God

Malachi probed a little deeper into the tribe of Judah when he identified their faithlessness to the precepts of God. Consider the words of verse 11: **"Judah has acted treacherously, and a detestable thing has been done in Israel and in Jerusalem. For Judah has profaned the LORD's sanctuary, which He loves, and has married the daughter of a foreign god."**

Judah's faithlessness is an abomination, a detestable act, to the Lord. By studying the Old Testament passages that dealt with detestable acts, like Leviticus 18:29, we understand that these acts deserved punishment and, ultimately, death. By using this specific word to describe their actions, Malachi was saying in essence, "You have done something despicable by profaning the sanctuary of the Lord, which will yield consequences for your disregard."

We can only speculate as to what their crime was in this context, but we do have other examples of similar judgments earlier in Israel's history that may shed a bit of light on what was happening in the temple. One such passage is Jeremiah 7, where the prophet described something that looks very similar to what was happening in the days of Malachi. Jeremiah asked, "Do you steal, murder, commit adultery, swear falsely, burn incense to Baal, and follow other gods that you have not known?" (Jer. 7:9). In this passage, their indictment was that they had profaned the Lord through theft, murder, adultery, and deceit. Worst of all, they chased after false gods—the ultimate betrayal of their covenantal relationship with God.

In Malachi we see yet another instance when Israel found itself in the crosshairs of a holy God. They had married worshipers of foreign deities.

Bronze figure of the
Canaanite god Baal
depicted as a warrior.
Found at Tyre, it dates
from 1400-1200 B.C.

They had divorced their first love—Yahweh. That phrase *foreign god* in verse 11 refers to any god other than the God of Israel, the one true God.

Some commentators would submit that the offense in view is idolatry, in which the priests were bowing down to pagan gods rather than to Yahweh. Idolatry is certainly an issue, but the text demands to be read in the context of physical, literal marriage. Whenever marriage is mentioned in Scripture in regards to God and Israel, God is always described as the bridegroom and Israel is always described as the bride. So Malachi was probably not talking about idolatry when he wrote that they **married the daughter** of false gods. He almost certainly must be addressing real marriage and real divorce. These priests were violating the sacred bonds of marriage, as declared by the Lord.

Why would they marry unbelievers when God strictly prohibited it in the Old Testament? When we consider that they had just come back into the promised land after being exiled, one obvious answer is that it was a matter of personal gain. One of the fastest ways to secure wealth was to marry into a wealthy family, so they put the precepts of God aside for personal profit. They began to intermarry with pagan women. They divorced the wives of their youth (v. 14) and they married unbelieving women.

God strictly forbade this in the Old Testament, not because He disregarded different races. His marital warning was not an issue of racial exclusivity. It was protection of His covenant people against idolatry. In Deuteronomy 7:3-4, God strictly, specifically outlined this for the people: "Do not intermarry with them. Do not give your daughters to their sons or take their daughters for your sons, because they will turn your sons away from Me to worship other gods. Then the LORD's anger will burn against you, and He will swiftly destroy you."

The apostle Paul, probably thinking of this same context of Deuteronomy, gave a similar charge in 2 Corinthians 6:15, when he wrote, "What agreement does Christ have with Belial? Or what does a believer have in common with an unbeliever?" He expressed rather pointedly that the problem with marrying an unbeliever isn't merely that they hold to a different religion; the problem with marrying an unbeliever has to do with marrying someone with a different worldview. They see the world differently than you do as a believer. Christians have a certain system, a lens through which we look at the world, and an unbeliever does not share that lens. Christians have a framework based on Christ by which they love and give. It shapes their time, their talents, and their investments. It shapes the way they raise their kids. It shapes the way they participate in organizations. It shapes their discipline and their dedication. And to unite oneself in marriage with someone who has a contradictory worldview will pose a tremendous temptation to abandon the one true God for other pursuits. This was true for Israel, and it is still true for Christians today.

Author John Piper presented a strong warning to young people about marriage: "If the choice of a marriage partner still lies before you, settle it in your mind right now never to marry anyone that does not love the Lord Jesus with all his or her heart."[1] Even dating an unbeliever will present a problem for born-again Christians. "Missionary dating," as it is called, seldom works because when emotions get involved and romance is in the air, the non-Christian is usually the one with more influence. Catherine Paxton described marriage as strands of a hair-braid. Paxton wrote,

> A braid appears to contain only two strands of hair. But it is impossible to create a braid with only two strands. If the two could be put together at all, they would quickly unravel. Herein lies the mystery: What looks like two strands requires a third. The third strand, though not immediately evident, keeps the strand tightly woven.... In a Christian marriage, God's presence, like the third strand in a braid, holds husband and wife together.[2]

Verse 12, a difficult verse to wrestle with, speaks to the consequences of being disobedient to the Lord. It brings to mind 1 Samuel 15. Saul, chosen to be the king, was given a pretty straightforward plan by God through the prophet Samuel. He said, "Now go and attack the Amalekites and completely destroy everything they have. Do not spare them. Kill men and women, children and infants, oxen and sheep, camels and donkeys" (v. 3).

The reason for such specific instruction and utter annihilation was solely because God didn't want His people distracted. He didn't want them influenced by unbelieving pagans. So Saul, acting as God's instrument of judgment, went into battle. He emerged victorious, destroying the Amalekites and following the plan, except for a few things. First, he took the spoils of the land for himself. Secondly, he took the Amalekite king and allowed him to remain alive. Thirdly, he took some of the cattle and sheep, surely thinking, "We don't want to get rid of this!"

When Samuel approached Saul and confronted him face to face, Saul said his reason for taking the sheep, cattle, and other items from the land was that they were going to be offered to the Lord. They were going to sacrifice the animals and were going to give them to the Lord.

---

1. John Piper, "Let None Be Faithless to the Wife of His Youth" (preached November 22, 1987; available from the Internet at http://www.desiringgod.org/sermons/let-none-be-faithless-to-the-wife-of-his-youth; accessed January 19, 2016).

2. *Sermons Illustrated* November/December 2008 (available on the Internet at *http://www.biblestudytools.com/pastor-resources/illustrations/11548558.html*; accessed January 19, 2016).

In verse 22, Samuel pierced Saul's heart with these words: "Does the LORD take pleasure in burnt offerings and sacrifices as much as in obeying the LORD? Look: to obey is better than sacrifice, to pay attention is better than the fat of rams."

The priests in Malachi's day had not learned this lesson. They neglected God's clear precepts and chased after foreign wives, thus their sacrifices were rejected.

Personal Reflection:

1. What do you think it means to profane God's sanctuary? How might we offend God in this way, even without a temple?

2. What things in your life might God be telling you to destroy, like Saul with the Amalekites? Are you holding back in any way?

Israel's Faithlessness to Their Marriage Partners

The third area in which the people were faithless was to their partners. Look at verse 13: **"You cover the LORD's altar with tears, with weeping and groaning, because He no longer respects your offerings or receives them gladly from your hands."** The first indictment is found in 2:11, the second one in 2:12, and the final one is found in 2:13.

The **tears** mentioned in this verse are from men who have divorced their wives to marry other women, and who now find themselves in the predicament that God no longer accepts their offerings. They are attempting to understand why the Lord has refused their offerings.

Did you catch the emotional anguish? They were **weeping and groaning.** But God would not accept their offerings. He had cut them off from His presence. The covenant that God made with His people is reflected in the covenantal nature of marriage, as we see throughout the Old Testament. We see the same warnings against abusing the marriage covenant in Proverbs 2 and Ezekiel 16. In the garden of Eden, God used identical covenantal language when He posited, "This is why a man leaves his father and mother and bonds with his wife, and they become one

flesh" (Gen. 2:24). Each person is to leave the influences of their past and create, together, a new one under the guidance of holy God.

Jesus gave credence to this idea in the New Testament:

> But from the beginning of creation God made them male and female. For this reason a man will leave his father and mother [and be joined to his wife], and the two will become one flesh. So they are no longer two, but one flesh. Therefore what God has joined together, man must not separate. (Mark 10:6-9)

What Malachi did was bring the marriage covenant full circle. He connected the covenant of marriage to their covenant with God. Effectively he said, "You men married your wives in a covenant. This is the same commitment you had with God."

But the men feigned innocence. Look at what they said in verse 14:

> "For what reason?" Because the LORD has been a witness between you and the wife of your youth. You have acted treacherously against her, though she was your marriage partner and your wife by covenant.

One Puritan commentator described what's happening in this verse in this way:

> The woman whom you have wronged was the companion of those earlier and brighter days of your life when, in the bloom of her young beauty she left her father's house and shared in your early struggles and rejoiced in your later success, who walked arm in arm with you along the pilgrimage of your life cheering you in its trials by her gentle ministry. And now when the bloom of her youth has faded and the friends of her youth have gone,

when her father and mother whom she left for you are in the grave, then you cruelly cast her off as a worn out worthless thing and insult her holiest affections by putting an idolater and a heathen in her place.[3]

We live in a day when divorce is not a last resort, but the first. Tom Brokaw, many years ago, spoke about the generation of men and women who lived through World War II, saying that, in general terms, it was the last generation to consider marriage a commitment and to rule out divorce as an option. Today is quite different: people think separation will be easier for their situation, but it often only causes more problems.

Friends, let me just challenge you briefly. Before a Christian should ever divorce, he or she should do everything in his or her power to make the marriage work. Remember that it is not just the covenant with your spouse that is at stake, it is also a covenant before the Lord. The people of Israel disregarded their marital covenants, and they found themselves under the wrath of their covenant God. Marriage was not intended merely to make us happy; it was meant to make us holy.

Personal Reflection:

1. Why is divorce contrary to the biblical idea of marriage as a covenant?

2. What are some practical difficulties to marrying someone who doesn't share your worldview? How might you be tempted to compromise or devalue the gospel?

3. Consider God's role in the covenant relationship between a man and a woman in marriage. How should that affect our approach to marriage as Christians?

---

3. Thomas V. Moore,. *Haggai and Malachi* .(New York: Banner of Truth Trust, 1960), 134.

Covenant Renewal Begins with Faithfulness to the Covenant of Marriage

Finally, Malachi delivered a challenge, a charge: "You men have been faithless to the precepts of God. You've been faithless to the people of God. You've been faithless to the partner of your marriage. But now I want you to follow the instructions of God." Look at verses 15-16:

> Didn't the one God make us with a remnant of His life-breath? And what does the One seek? A godly offspring. So watch yourselves carefully, and do not act treacherously against the wife of your youth. "If he hates and divorces his wife," says the LORD God of Israel, "he covers his garment with injustice," says the LORD of Hosts. Therefore, watch yourselves carefully, and do not act treacherously.

The command to **watch yourselves** is a means of protection. It is a practical command for us to monitor the negative, unspiritual information that we receive from unbelievers. We need to monitor who is speaking into our lives about our biblical commitments, particularly the covenant we have made with our spouses.

If I had a strangely shaped mole on my leg, I wouldn't go to a salesman friend of mine and ask, "Hey Mike, can you come look at this thing?" He might bend down and say, "Wow, that thing is asymmetrical, very discolored. It's got spider veins shooting off from the side. Looks fine to me. Just put some antibiotic ointment on it. You'll be fine in the morning." But would I follow that advice? No! I would never go to Mike in the first place! I'd go to a professional doctor because I want someone who knows what he is talking about to diagnose my problem.

So why would we ever listen to unbelievers giving us spiritual advice about a covenant we've made with God? Wouldn't we go to our brothers and sisters in Christ and let them speak into this relationship reflecting Christ and His bride, the Church?

The University of Chicago supported this idea in the secular realm many years ago. Researchers conducted a study on people who stayed together and people who divorced, and they found out that couples in the midst of struggle had a superior chance of staying together if the friends around them encouraged them to stay together, and if those friends were married themselves. Couples in turmoil had a higher risk of divorce when many of their friends around them were divorced and were bitter toward their ex-husbands or ex-wives.

Paul said that bad company corrupts good character (see 1 Cor. 15:33). Who are your closest friends? Whose advice is central in your life?

LEARNING ACTIVITY

Godly Fruit

Paul identified the fruit of the Spirit (Gal. 5:22-23) as:

Love	Joy	Peace
Patience	Kindness	Goodness
Faith	Gentleness	Self-control

What does all of this fruit have in common? That is, what do they describe?

Are they attitudes? Actions? Internal qualities that stay hidden or external qualities that can be seen?

If they can be seen, by whom?

Who benefits from these fruit in our lives? Who is hurt if these fruit are not evident in our lives?

Malachi 2:16 proclaims exactly what God thinks of divorce. He equates it with **injustice** and again warns His people to **watch yourselves carefully** so as to **not act treacherously** in the matter of divorce. Second, we see in the structure of the text that emphasis is added to whatever is being said with God's name on the front **(LORD God of Israel)** and back **(LORD of Hosts)** ends of it. God bookends this truth with His signature. He says, "You can take this to the bank. This is something I don't want to happen. When you cover your **garment with injustice,** it's a deplorable act. Don't do it."

Personal Reflection:

1. What does divorce say about the gospel of Jesus? How does this passage relate to Ephesians 5:21-33?

2. How should we respond to divorce in the culture? In the church?

Conclusion: Christ as the Faithful Bridegroom Relentlessly Pursuing His Bride, the Church

It is easy to take some of these words and begin pointing fingers at other people who may have experienced divorce. However, let the record show: divorce is not the unpardonable sin. God does not hate divorce any worse than He hates any other sin; all sin is deplorable to the Lord. So what do you do if you've been divorced? You repent, ask God's forgiveness, and move on because failure need not be final in the believer's life.

Let me remind you, brother or sister who isn't divorced—before you begin to point the finger at another person who is divorced—look at the landscape of your own life to determine ways you have failed and places you have fallen. Who can stand in the presence of our holy God? If we listen to what God's Word is saying here, whether we're remarried or we're married for the first time, we stay together to the end. That's the first point of application.

Finally, we must look at the One who was faithful, Jesus Christ. While Israel chased after other gods, Jesus remained faithful to the God of the covenant, and relentlessly pursued His Bride. Though she was unfaithful to Him, He remained in pursuit, all the way to the cross, so He might purchase her with His own blood. This is the story of the gospel, it is the standard for faithfulness, it is the soaring wings of redemption, and it is the only hope we have to mend all of our broken relationships.

Personal Reflection:

1. How can we guard ourselves and our marriages from imploding?

2. What precepts of God do you tend to take lightly? What does your attitude toward these reflect about your attitude toward the Lord?

LEARNING ACTIVITY

Be on Guard

Malachi warns to "watch yourselves carefully, and do not act treacherously" (Mal. 2:16). Identify as many ways as you can in which we can guard ourselves from the temptation to sin by acting treacherously against other believers, especially our spouses.

CHAPTER FOUR

Where Is the God of Justice?

MALACHI 2:17–3:5

his passage starts with an expression of exasperation. **"You have wea-ried the Lord with your words,"** said Malachi. The Israelites had com-plained, doubted, put up repeated fronts of ignorance, but the Lord was tired of their disrespect. In this passage, God declared that the people had the answers to the coy questions they asked. They would see the Lord work, but it would not be in the way they desired. God would fulfill His covenant, but it would come through judgment and a promised messenger. In essence, the Lord took the people to court.

Accusing God of Injustice for Allowing the Wicked to Prosper

In Malachi 2:17, the people of God questioned the Lord's justice, thereby, prompt-ing Him to give them an answer to their objections. We witness three stages of God's interrogation. First, there is an accusation. God accused the people through His servant, Malachi, when He said, "You have wearied the Lord." The word *wea-ried* describes exhaustion from physical labor. It also carries the connotation of being an "annoyance." It is to be agitated by something or someone; in this case, the people of Israel had aggravated God.

Second, there is a rebuttal. The people responded defensively to Malachi's ac-cusation from the Lord. And why would we expect anything different from them? The people had repeatedly pleaded ignorance up to this point. They responded, **"How have we wearied Him?"** either out of obliviousness or feigned innocence. Either way, they were prompting the Lord to explain to them precisely what they had done.

You're Making Me Tired!

All of us at times are tempted to come to God with questions or complaints that are selfish or rebellious in nature. Take a moment and think of a time or times when you were angry or upset with God. What were some of the questions you asked?

What were your complaints?

Do you think perhaps you made Him "weary" with your words? Explain.

Then finally, there's a validation in the text. Malachi was explicit about their wearisome ways. The people had effectively been saying, **"Everyone who does what is evil is good in the Lord's sight, and He is pleased with them."** Or by asking, **"Where is the God of justice?"**

It would seem as though the people were becoming impatient because of the rampant immorality and political corruption in Israel. They were saying to God, in essence, "God, why are You making the wicked prosper? Do You find joy in their transgressions? Where is Your justice?" Through reflection on the Law and their ancestral history, the people of Israel should have realized that God is always just. Deuteronomy 28 makes it clear that the people of the covenant will receive blessings if they obey and curses if they do not, but justice comes according to God's timetable and not that of the Israelites:

> Now if you faithfully *obey* the Lord your God and are careful to follow all His commands I am giving you today, the Lord your God will

put you far above all the nations of the earth. All these blessings will come and overtake you, because you obey the LORD your God: You will be blessed in the city and blessed in the country. Your descendants will be blessed, and your land's produce, and the offspring of your livestock, including the young of your herds and the newborn of your flocks. Your basket and kneading bowl will be blessed. You will be blessed when you come in and blessed when you go out. But if you do *not* obey the LORD your God by carefully following all His commands and statutes I am giving you today, all these curses will come and overtake you: You will be cursed in the city and cursed in the country. Your basket and kneading bowl will be cursed. Your descendants will be cursed, and your land's produce, the young of your herds, and the newborn of your flocks. You will be cursed when you come in and cursed when you go out. (Deut. 28:1-6,15-19, emphasis mine)

Questioning how the wicked can receive blessing is found throughout the Old Testament. In fact, five books ask the question directly: Job 21:7; Psalm 82:2; Ecclesiastes 7:15;

The 1st century A.D. bema (tribunal) where Paul stood before Gallio in Corinth (Acts 18:12-17).

Jeremiah 12:1; and Habakkuk 1:13. Many are still asking the same question today: How can the wicked prosper?

In this passage, God was not interested in giving an explanation for why He gives blessings to sinners. However, God did take the opportunity to display in stark detail the hypocrisy of His people. The Israelites pointed the finger at God when they should have pointed it back at themselves. Through their interrogation of God, they opened a door for God's critique of their lives and lifestyle. Be careful next time you question God. He may have a series of questions for you in return.

Personal Reflection:

1. Describe a time when you looked around and thought the wicked were prospering and the righteous were being mistreated? How did you respond?

2. Have you wearied the Lord with your sin in the past? Explain. How does this text warn us against such sin?

God Defends His Justice and Makes a Promise

God promised to send His appointed messenger to announce His coming judgment: **See, I am going to send My messenger, and he will clear the way before Me** (Mal. 3:1). Who is this messenger? We see in Malachi 4:5 that Elijah is this forerunner. Elijah was the one who was to come and prepare the way of the Lord. Isaiah 40:3-5 uses the same word "prepare" or "clear obstacles":

A voice of one crying out: Prepare the way of the Lord in the wilderness; make a straight highway for our God in the desert. Every valley will be lifted up, and every mountain and hill will be leveled; the uneven ground will become smooth and the rough places, a plain. And the glory of the Lord will appear, and all humanity together will see it, for the mouth of the Lord has spoken.

Each of the four Gospel writers associate the messenger of these verses with the ministry of John the Baptist (see Matt. 3:1-4; Mark 1:1-4; Luke 3:1-6; John 1:6-8,19-

23). The question arises, "How did John the Baptizer prepare the way for the coming of the Lord?" In the first century, and even centuries before that, some Jews believed a person prepared the way of the Lord with his or her body. That is, a person could live an upright life by removing distractions or impediments that would appeal to the body but hinder holiness. The Essene sect, generally associated with the Qumran community, exemplified this belief.

Many scholars suggest John the Baptist was influenced by the Essenes. There are a number of similarities between the Essenes and John. First, like the Essenes, John the Baptist separated himself from the rest of society by living and preaching in the wilderness. His father Zechariah was a priest, so he could have claimed his spot to work in the temple. Instead, he battled the conditions of the wilderness to preach righteousness. The wilderness referred to in the Bible was a proper desert. It presented a hard, impoverished existence, which demonstrated John's unconcern, like the Essenes, with the things of the world or the comforts for the body. He was laser focused on preparing the way for the coming Messiah.

Second, the Essenes were known for their ritual baptisms. In order to maintain their cleanliness and ritual holiness before the Lord, the Essenes baptized themselves in a mikveh, that is, a purification bath. The washing was

The Essene city of Qumran dates from the late Hellenistic to the early Roman period.

ILLUSTRATOR PHOTO/BOB SCHATZ (9/5/13)

necessary for the induction of a new member. The baptism was self-adminis-tered with the individual going into the water three times with their arms folded across their chest.

Although there are many similarities between John the Baptist and the Essenes, there are a number of differences that must be addressed. First, although the Bap-tizer separated himself from society, he eventually emerged from the desert. The Essenes, on the other hand, remained in the desert until the Roman military mas-sacred them in A.D. 68. Second, John the Baptist baptized people once, in response to their repentance. In this way, he prepared the way of the Lord. The Essenes, on the other hand, baptized themselves repeatedly: before they ate, worshiped, prayed, copied literature, and so forth. Thirdly, and most importantly, John the Baptist recognized Jesus as the Messiah, whereas the Essene community awaited the resurrection and return of their "Teacher of Righteousness"—whose name has not survived the passing of history—and died waiting. They never put faith in Je-sus as the promised Son of God.

If this messenger who was to prepare the way was supposed to draw our atten-tion to John the Baptist, then what was God talking about when He said, **"Then the Lord you seek will suddenly come to His temple, the Messenger of the covenant you desire—see, He is coming"?** The temple in reference in the text is the second temple, the one that was built by Zerubbabel, the same one talked about by Haggai and Zechariah. This was the temple of Nehemiah's day when he rebuilt the walls around Jerusalem. And it is the same foundational structure—though greatly ex-panded by Herod the Great—into which Jesus entered a week before His death to

cleanse and purge unrighteous business practices on the part of the leaders (Matt. 21:12-13).

So who would be the approaching **Messenger of the covenant?** He is the Christ, Jesus, the Lord incarnate. Jesus' entry into the temple precincts during the week of His passion was the fulfillment of this prophecy. John the Baptizer prepared the way of the Lord by promoting the repentance of Israel. With the scene set, God, through His Son, entered His temple and evaluated His people.

The connection between 3:1 and 2:17 is marked with a single Hebrew word. Malachi 2:17 states that the people claimed: **Everyone who does what is evil is good in the Lord's sight, and He is pleased with them.** The people claimed that God delighted in evil. But what God showed them is that the Messiah, **of the covenant you desire** (the Hebrew word translated **desire** in 3:1 is a form of the word rendered **pleased** in 2:17) was coming not to bless the Israelites. Rather, He **suddenly** was coming for their condemnation. "Suddenly" does not merely mean "quickly." "Suddenly" here refers to the way He will come: The Lord is coming at a moment the Israelites do not expect and implies an ominous situation. It reminds us of how Christ will return a second time when people least expect Him: "For you yourselves know very well that the Day of the Lord will come just like a thief in the night" (1 Thess. 5:2).

We see this same language in Matthew 21:12-13 (see also Mark 11:15-18; Luke 19:45-47; John 2:14-16). In that passage, the Jewish leaders were going through the routine of exchanging money in the temple. The merchants were corrupt and meeting in the court of the Gentiles in the temple complex, and thereby keeping foreigners from worshiping the Lord of all. With whip in hand, Jesus overturned the tables and said, "It is written, My house will be called a house of prayer. But you are making it a den of thieves." In essence, what He was saying when He did this was, "This is my Father's house and I'm claiming ownership of it. This is a foreshadowing of the cleansing that will come by My Father." God warned His people of His coming in Malachi, but they did not heed His warning. God is both the sender of the messenger and the One coming to purify the people.

A mikveh from the second temple period just below southern steps in Jerusalem. New believers would have been baptized here on the day of Pentecost.

Personal Reflection:

1. How is it comforting to know that God will come to judge the world? How should we Christians anticipate this judgment?

2. There are two messengers reflected in this text. What are the roles of each one, and how are they fulfilled in the New Testament?

God's Promised Vindication Begins with the Purification of Israel's Priestly Leadership

We have seen the people's interrogation of God. Then we saw God promise that He would send His Messenger. Now, we see the purification of God's priests. God did not begin by judging and purifying the common Israelite; He began by purifying the once-holy priesthood. Read Malachi 3:2-3:

> But who can endure the day of His coming? And who will be able to stand when He appears? For He will be like a refiner's fire and like cleansing lye. He will be like a refiner and purifier of silver; He will purify the sons of Levi and refine them like gold and silver. Then they will present offerings to the Lord in righteousness.

This passage cannot be about Jesus' first coming, since Jesus did not come to re-fine but redeem. Jesus came to give His life up as a sacrifice for all of mankind. He came to emancipate sinners and to establish His kingdom. At His second coming, though, He will act as judge and purifier. Martin Luther said, "There are only two days on my calendar: This day and that Day."[1] For the Israelites, there were only two days on the calendar: today and the Day of the Lord. In the same manner, there are only two days that should matter to every believer: today and the day Jesus returns to test our worth. There is a day coming when the only thing that will really matter is what you and I did for Christ. The great cricket player turned

---

1. Fries, Rummage, and Gallaty, 245.

missionary, C. T. Studd, said it well: "Only one life 'twill soon be past. Only what's done for Christ will last."[2]

This passage is not a warning of destruction but a promise of purification. Malachi assured the people that the Messiah would bring with Him the **refiner's fire.** What is a refiner's fire? It is a fire that purifies precious metals. Gold, silver, copper, or another like metal is heated until it melts into a liquid state. The dross or impurities float to the top where the refiner can skim them off. Once the process is over, the metal is without impurities and, therefore, of greater worth and usefulness.

For Christians there are two forms of purification. The first takes place on earth, where God's divine instrument for molding and making us into the image of Christ often involves pain and suffering. This is made vivid in Hebrews 12:5-6,11:

> And you have forgotten the exhortation that addresses you as sons: My son, do not take the Lord's discipline lightly or faint when you are reproved by Him, for the Lord disciplines the one He loves and punishes every son He receives. No discipline seems enjoyable at the time, but painful. Later on, however, it yields the fruit of peace and righteousness to those who have been trained by it.

God also often uses other people to shape us into the image of Christ. Proverbs 27:17 states, "Iron sharpens iron, and one man sharpens another."

Replica of a copper smelting furnace as found in situ at Timna. The slag pit in the front is flanked by long blocks of stone; dates to the twelfth century B.C.

ILLUSTRATOR PHOTO/ KRISTEN HILLER/ ERETZ ISRAEL MUSEUM/ TEL AVIV (45/2141)

2. Charles Studd, *http://sermonindex.net/modules/newbb/viewtopic.php?topic_id=30864&forum=34* [Internet] (accessed February 5, 2016).

"Iron sharpens iron,
and one man
sharpens another."

— PROVERBS 27:17

People are divine instruments in God's plan to grow us spiritually. He uses friends, neighbors, co-workers, bosses, and family members. He will use your spouse, your children, your customers, your pastor, music minister, and Sunday School teachers. He can even utilize your enemies and antagonists to bring about change in your life.

In addition to using people, God uses circumstances to help us grow. Romans 8:28 reminds us of this: "We know that all things work together for the good of those who love God: those who are called according to His purpose." God works all things together for good. God uses financial difficulties, physical ailments, trials, tribulation, persecution, setbacks, even the weather to mold us into the image of His Son.

God also uses spiritual disciplines to develop us into the image of His Son. People and circumstances affect us from outside of ourselves, but spiritual disciplines transform us from within. Unlike outside circumstances, you and I have complete control over exercising the spiritual disciplines in our lives. Instead of waiting for God to send some circumstance or individual to assist in conforming us to the image of His Son, we have complete control over the frequency and intensity of our spiritual exercise.

We are being purged here on earth from impurities, but we will finally be purified at the bema seat or "tribunal of Christ" (2 Cor. 5:10). Every believer will experience testing in this life, as through fire, in order to be glorified. Read 1 Corinthians 3:11-15:

> For no one can lay any other foundation than what has been laid down. That foundation is Jesus Christ. If anyone builds on that foundation with gold, silver, costly stones, wood, hay, or straw, each one's work will become obvious, for the day will disclose it, because it will be revealed by fire; the fire will test the quality of each one's work. If anyone's work that he has built survives, he will receive a reward. If anyone's work is burned up, it will be lost, but he will be saved; yet it will be like an escape through fire.

Only what glorifies our Lord will stand the test of God's fire. The sin nature with which we have been cursed will be destroyed and we will be conformed to the image of Christ.

LEARNING ACTIVITY

Cleanse Me, O God

According to the writer, God uses three areas to bring cleansing in our lives. In the space below, list an example of how God has used each of those areas in your life. Look for an opportunity to share your experiences with someone else.

Other People–

Circumstances–

Spiritual Disciplines–

It is important, therefore, for us to examine daily the things that we are doing for the Lord. That is why the Scripture constantly reminds its readers to examine themselves. Examination of works today is better than elimination of blessings tomorrow. So praise God for His purging us through suffering. The purpose of God for your life is to conform you into the image of His Son Jesus. His goal is not to make you happy, although joy is a by-product of an intimate relationship with Christ. His goal is not to preserve your health or give you wealth. His goal is to mold and shape you into the likeness of His Son. James encouraged the believers dispersed throughout the region with the joy that comes through trials: "Consider it a great joy, my brothers, whenever you experience various trials, knowing that the testing of your faith produces endurance. But endurance must do its complete work, so that you may be mature and complete, lacking nothing" (Jas. 1:2-4).

Personal Reflection:

1. What does it mean to only have two days on your calendar: this day and that Day? How can this help you keep perspective in this life?

2. What is the purpose of God's purifying process in our lives? Read 1 Peter 1:6-7 for more insight.

God's Promised Vindication Culminates with the Judgment of His People Israel

There is a final aspect to the text. We have seen the interrogation of God, the promise of the coming Messenger, and the purification of the priests of God. Now we witness the examination of Israel by God, the righteous Judge. Look at Malachi 3:5:

> "I will come to you in judgment, and I will be ready to witness against sorcerers and adulterers; against those who swear falsely; against those who oppress the widow and the fatherless, and cheat the wage earner; and against those who deny justice to the foreigner. They do not fear Me," says the LORD of Hosts.

God expanded the purification from the priests to all Israel. Not just anyone would be called to witness against the sins of the people. God would summons a star witness: Himself. God is the only One who can be trusted to testify as the honest and discerning witness to the transgressions of His people. He charged the nation for participating in four prohibited acts, each of which stem from a lack of fear toward the Lord: sorcery, adultery, lying, and those who oppress vulnerable members of society (**widow ... fatherless ... wage earner ... foreigner).**

Sorcery refers to the act of looking to other places, whether to foreign gods or simple magic, for power and might. The people were looking to something other than their covenant God, which reveals a lack of respect for Him. Likewise, both adultery and lying were explicitly prohibited in the Ten Commandments. The covenant people, marked by the fear of the Lord, were to be a people of marital faithfulness and truth-telling, just like their God. In exposing these sins, too, the people's hearts were on display.

By oppressing the most vulnerable in society, Israel revealed that they had forgotten where they had come from. Throughout the Old Testament, God reminded Israel to care for the helpless. The reason for this was because Israel had been a helpless nation in Egypt, yet the Lord set His heart to care for them. An example of this expectation is seen in Exodus 22: "You must not exploit a foreign resident or oppress him, since you were foreigners in the land of Egypt. You must not mistreat any widow or fatherless child. If you do mistreat them, they will no doubt cry to Me, and I will certainly hear their cry" (vv. 21-23). In oppressing the weak, the Israelites showed that they had forgotten the grace the Lord had shown to them. God blessed them to be a blessing to others. They were made different to make a difference as lights to a dark world.

The fear of the Lord preserves us for the day of judgment. It teaches us to live in light of God's grace and mercy. Without this proper fear, we forget the radical nature of the good news and we turn away from God. If we lack fear, we may be judged through fire to be without worth, showing that we never truly belonged to God in faith. However, God's Word contains a promise to those who have turned from sin and put their faith in Christ. John in the final book of the Bible stated, "The victor will be dressed in white clothes, and I will never erase his name from the book of life" (Rev. 3:5).

Conclusion: Christ as the Promised Messenger of the Covenant

It's easy to point a finger at the injustice of our country, unbelievers, or enemies, while we turn blind eyes and deaf ears to our own shortcomings. Jesus warned His disciples about the futility of doing the same when He said,

> Do not judge, so that you won't be judged. For with the judgment you use, you will be judged, and with the measure you use, it will be measured to you. Why do you look at the speck in your brother's eye but don't notice the log in your own eye? Or how can you say to your brother, "Let me take the speck out of your eye," and look, there's a log in your eye? Hypocrite! First take the log out of your eye, and then you will see clearly to take the speck out of your brother's eye. (Matt. 7:1-5)

The Book of Malachi begins with Israel pointing the finger at other nations, but ends with God pointing the finger at them. God in essence said, "Don't worry about those outside the nation of Israel, look at those within. And start with yourself." Don't say, "What about them?" Instead, say, "What about me?" Be careful of pointing fingers at others, you might have a few pointed back at you.

The good news of Malachi 2:17–3:5 is that there was a **Messenger of the covenant** who would come. He upheld the covenant between God and Israel in His life, and He sealed the covenant in His blood at the cross. Every time Christians take the Lord's Supper, we proclaim that the Messenger has come, and He will come again. Jesus said as much in Mark 14:22-25. We look back at His faithfulness, resting in the promise of His grace. In court before God, His blood is our plea. And by His power, looking forward to His return, we live with the fear of the Lord, doing good works that will be tested and approved, fully pleasing to God, just like our King Jesus.

Personal Reflection:

1. Why do you think the Lord started with the priests and then moved to the people? Where else can we see this principle in Scripture?

2. What acts do you do that reveal a lack of "fear of the Lord"? Examine your heart and consider why you still chase after these things. What do you discover?

3. If Christians are in Christ and are fully accepted by God through Him, why are we still judged on our works? Is this inconsistent? Explain.

CHAPTER FIVE

How Can We Return?

MALACHI 3:6-12

Introduction: The Unchanging Nature of Israel's Covenant God

"Because I, Yahweh, have not changed, you descendants of Jacob have not been destroyed. Since the days of your fathers, you have turned from My statutes; you have not kept them. Return to Me, and I will return to you,' says the LORD of Hosts"** (Mal. 3:6-7).

The words God spoke here are intensely comforting, particularly the final part of the passage. Though the Israelites had failed, God had not changed, and this was the very foundation of His promise of restoration.

Israel's Checkered History and the Reality of Her Rebellion

The first thing we notice in this text is the reality of Israel's rebellion. In 3:5, God left the people wondering by saying through His messenger Malachi, "I will come to you in judgment." That is, "I'm through with playing games. Now, I'm handing down sentences." He followed up with this phrase: **"Because I, Yahweh, have not changed, you descendants of Jacob have not been destroyed."** God was saying, in essence, "You have sinned and you deserve judgment. But I'm going to extend my mercy to you because of the promise I made to your father, Jacob."

By using the terminology **descendants of Jacob** God departed from His usual pattern. Normally, the people were referred to as the children of "Israel." In place of calling them "Israelites," God addressed them as "Jacobites." If you remember, when God gave Jacob His promise in Genesis, He changed Jacob's name. He declared, "Your name will no longer be Jacob .... It will be Israel because you have struggled with God and with men and have prevailed" (Gen. 32:28).

When God referred to the Israelites as the children of "Jacob," He used the name of their father before the divine blessing was bestowed. He reminded the people that even though they were faithless, He would remain faithful to them, as He had been to their father, Jacob. But even in this text, reminding them of the reality of their rebellion against their covenant God ensured that restoration was possible through Him.

Once again, the nations of Israel's relationship with God can be pictured as the covenant relationship of marriage. Even though they strayed from Him, even though they deserted Him, and even though they prostituted their bodies to other gods by engaging in idolatrous worship, God remained by their side. He never left them or turned His back on them because He had made a promise. He always comes through with His promises. Are you starting to see a pattern in the text? The Hebrew language stresses a point through repetition of thought. Without the use of punctuation marks, authors emphasized a truth by repeating it. For example, God is not merely holy. He is holy, holy, holy.

Couples, in a similar manner, make promises to each other before God at their wedding. "I promise to stay by your side

Located at the intersection of major cross-roads, the region around Bethel was heavily traveled for much of the Old Testament Era. It was here that God renewed His promise to Jacob through a dream of angels ascending and descending from heaven.

ILLUSTRATOR PHOTO/ BOB SCHATZ (18/27/7)

as your faithful spouse in sickness and in health, in joy and in sorrow, in the good times and the bad." When a husband, who is a picture of Christ, abandons his wife, he unknowingly declares that God deserts His people. Likewise, when a wife, who is a picture of the church, deserts her husband, she unknowingly declares that Christ is not satisfying enough for His people. When a person abandons the God of the universe through idolatry, it is infinitely magnified.

Do you feel like you are far from the Lord right now? Do you feel like you have turned your back on God? If so, you can return to Him now, because God gives us the recipe for return and will always be there when we call upon His name.

Personal Reflection:

When was a time you thought you were too sinful for God to forgive you? How has He shown Himself faithful to His covenant through Christ in your situation?

God's Indictment of Israel
for Withholding Their Tithes and Offerings

In the verses that follow, the Lord offered His road map to reconciliation. Reconciliation is always offered, but the people must return to the Lord and cease their selfish, rebellious ways. Malachi presented the Lord's case:

"Since the days of your fathers, you have turned from My statutes; you have not kept them. Return to Me, and I will return to you," says the LORD of Hosts. But you ask: "How can we return?" "Will a man rob God? Yet you are robbing Me!" You ask: "How do we rob You?" (Mal. 3:7-8)

The people asked, "God, how shall we return to You?" This is not a question of clarification, it is one of disputation. The New Living Translation translates the people's exclamation well: "How can we return when we've never gone away?" It is as if they were saying, "God, what are You talking about?"

Taking Assessment

People traditionally set New Year's resolutions during the first part of a new year. They take an assessment of their lives and determine ways in which they would like (or need) to improve during the coming year. Take an assessment of your relationship with God. Which of the following best describes your current position in relation to God?

___ As snug as a bug in a rug.

___ Lord, I'm coming home.

___ As up and down as a yo-yo.

___ Drifting away.

___ Never the twain shall meet.

Explain your answer.

The word **return** can also be translated as *repent*. It's an about-face in military talk. It is more than a mere orientation. Repentance is the restoration of a relationship and a reconfirmation of commitment to someone. In this case, the Israelites were called to renew their relationship with God. When you are unaware of how you've gotten to where you are, returning to where you started is rather hard. If you are walking through the woods and you do not take record of your steps, it's often very difficult to retrace them. How much more difficult it is when you do not even realize you are lost! The children of Israel, God's chosen people, demonstrated themselves to be in that exact situation. They stood before holy God and said, "God, how can we return? We aren't even lost!"

Before you scoff, realize that it is just as easy for us to fall into the same trap today. We may say, "Far from God? I am not far from God! I go to church every week! My kids are in a Christian school! How can you say I am far from God?" God may reply to you in a similar way to how He replied to the people of Jacob: "You do not think you are far from Me, but you are far from Me." It takes consistent and deep personal evaluation to determine how far we are from the Lord. Fortunately, for this process, Christians have the inner-working of the Holy Spirit. But the Israelites were not as privileged. For them, God spoke in His Spirit through the prophets. Through Malachi, God put His finger on the pulse of the people's rebellion. They asked in what way they were far from God, so God answered them:

> By not making the payments of the tenth and the contributions. You are suffering under a curse, yet you—the whole nation—are still robbing Me. Bring the full tenth into the storehouse so that there may be food in My house. (vv. 8-10)

God previously had challenged the Israelites for their poor sacrifices, their lack of worship, their idolatry, and their faithlessness. But here He identified the heart of the problem, which was a problem of their heart that found expression through their misappropriation of funds. The problem was not what the people possessed. Rather, it was what they did with their possessions. They were withholding the proper tithes from God, to which God responded, "You have an abundance. Why? Because I am the One who blessed you. Nonetheless, you are not giving Me your best. You are giving Me what is left." Look back at Malachi 1:8. There, God expressed His expectation that the people offer Him their best. But notice what they give: "When you present a blind animal for sacrifice, is it not wrong? And when you present a lame or sick animal, is it not wrong?" God said, "I want a perfect, unblemished, pure sacrifice. Instead, you offer those that are lame or sick that you wouldn't offer to your governor."

The Israelites' lack of financial worship was not the problem in itself, but was instead an indication of their wicked hearts. Remember what Malachi said in 1:13: "'You bring stolen, lame, or sick animals. You bring this as an offering! Am I to accept that from your hands?' asks the LORD." The Israelites looked at their flock and said, "We have savings here in the form of a goat. We have a nice investment in her. She's beautiful. But this scrawny-looking thing here ... we can give that one to God." We see that in the first section of Malachi, God dealt with the quality of their offering. In the second half of Malachi, He dealt with the quantity of their offering. In both sections, though, their adulterous hearts were revealed before God.

If we try to shrug off the message of these passages or try to gloss over it by saying, "It's really not about money," then we stumble. It is absolutely about money. God is showing us that you can always determine the pulse of individuals by putting a finger on their pocket books. You can always determine where a person's heart is by evaluating his or her bank account statements. We may not like to talk about money, but money talks a lot about us. And for both Israel and for us, our wallets betray us.

Personal Reflection:

1. Sometime people assume they are in a right relationship with God when they are not. What types of things other than Christ do we often look to as evidence that we are Christians?

2. What do your spending habits reveal about your heart? Explain.

On Tithes and Offerings

The tenth or **the full tenth** often appears in other Bible versions as the more familiar church word "tithe." In either case, according to the context of Malachi, it referred to 10 percent. All that God was requiring of His people was the lowest amount that was required under the Law. Ultimately, though, the Jews were required to give above 10 percent. For instance, the Israelites were required to contribute money toward festivals and feasts, as well as to the sacrifices in the temple. If everything that was required of the people's giving were totaled together, faithful Israelites gave more than 10 percent of what they owned for the purpose of maintaining the worship of God in the temple.

Scholars are divided as to whether we as Christians under the New Covenant are required to follow the Old Testament rule of tithing a tenth of our resources. There are a considerable number who suggest that we are to tithe a tenth of our goods, and that the church is considered a storehouse, a replacement for the temple. Against this assertion, there are those who claim that we are not obligated to give a tenth of our income; rather, we have no obligations since we are under grace. This reasoning states that because of the sacrifice of the Lord Jesus Christ, we are not obligated to give a tenth of anything; we are free to give whatever we want to give.

There is not enough space available here to unpack this idea fully, but it is necessary to say two things before moving ahead. First, under the auspices of the covenant of grace, grace always demands more than the Law. This is demonstrated from a quick examination of the Sermon on the Mount in the Gospel of Matthew. Jesus told His audience, "You have heard that it was said to our ancestors, Do not murder, and whoever murders will be subject to judgment. But I tell you, everyone who is angry with his brother will be subject to judgment. And whoever says to his brother, 'Fool!' will be subject to the Sanhedrin. But whoever says, 'You moron!' will be subject to hellfire" (Matt. 5:21-22). Jesus consistently raised the bar. Likewise, Jesus said, "You have heard that it was said, Do not commit adultery. But I tell you, everyone who looks at a woman to lust for her has already committed adultery with her in his heart" (vv. 27-28).

Therefore, grace never expects less; it always demands more. While we are not required to give a tenth based on the Old Testament Law, since we are not under the Law, the question arises, "Should we give any less than the Old Testament saints did since we are under grace and not under the Law?" The answer is that we should give more, as a spiritual act of worship. Ten percent can be used as a guide for giving, much like training wheels on a bicycle guide those learning to ride. We should seek to show our worship to the Lord through our giving and, therefore, should never be satisfied with presenting the bare minimum.

The second challenge to grace-inspired giving is that we should give out of the abundance God has given us, but we rarely feel like giving. When we are left to our own devices, and we are given the freedom to determine what we can and should give, few ever give as we should. We should not give to God because we are under obligation to tithe, we should tithe because we love our Maker and Savior, and want to give a portion of what He has bestowed upon us to Him.

We can agree on two principles related to giving. The first is that everything you and I own has come to us by God. Therefore, let us begin to look at what we have not as our resources—that is, not as things we have amassed by ourselves—but as resources we are borrowing from God. These resources are not to be considered as those things for which we have worked, although we have worked for them. These are gifts that God has bestowed upon us. He has commissioned us to be stewards of the resources and the blessings He has extended to us. If God owns everything, we will one day give an account to Him for what we have done with His possessions. Therefore, we should begin to ponder how well we would fare after His audit.

The second principle related to giving that we should all agree about is that we are all stewards of the Lord's money. We should each think about how we are stewarding that money in our relationships with other kingdom-bound people.

In this light, every one of us can be placed into one of two categories. Luke 18 and 19 describe two men who were diametrically opposed to one another in character. The first one is the rich young ruler:

> A ruler asked Him, "Good Teacher, what must I do to inherit eternal life?" "Why do you call Me good?" Jesus asked him. "No one is good but One—God. You know the commandments: Do not commit adultery; do not murder; do not steal; do not bear false witness; honor your father and mother." "I have kept all these from my youth," he said. When Jesus heard this, He told him, "You still lack one thing: Sell all that you have and distribute it to the poor, and you will have treasure in heaven. Then come, follow Me." After he heard this, he became extremely sad, because he was very rich. (Luke 18:18-23)

In the story of the rich young ruler, we see a man who had been entrusted with much but gave little. That is, we witness an example of a man who tried to serve two masters, with the result that he demonstrated his allegiance not to God, but to money.

In the very next chapter—and I don't think it is any accident that we see these two polar opposite stories within one chapter of each other—is the story of Zacchaeus. Jesus, having seen Zacchaeus up in a tree, told Zacchaeus in essence, "Let's go to your house. We are going to fellowship." As Jesus spoke words of life to him, Zacchaeus became convicted about his greed:

> But Zacchaeus stood there and said to the Lord, "Look, I'll give half of my possessions to the poor, Lord! And if I have extorted anything from anyone, I'll pay back four times as much!" "Today salvation has come to this house," Jesus told him, "because he too is a son of Abraham. For the Son of Man has come to seek and to save the lost." (Luke 19:8-10)

What a great comparison of two sinners! One man repented; one man retreated. One man was saved; one man was separated. Something like this comparison is taking place in the Book of Malachi among the people of God. Malachi was not necessarily calling out those who had been faithfully

giving, asking them to give more; Malachi was calling out those who gave less than they should. He was calling out those who haphazardly gave. He was calling out those who were writing checks without worshiping. Giving is an act of spiritual worship to the Lord.

Remember, a closed hand cannot receive a blessing. With a generous, open hand, you are opening yourself up to receive God's best. We don't give to receive. We give because we have already received all things in Jesus Christ. If God doesn't give you another thing in this world, He has blessed you enough with salvation in His Son. With a rebellious, closed hand, you declare your trust in yourself and not in God.

Personal Reflection:

1. What does it mean that "grace never expects less; it always expects more"? Why would this be true?

2. Why do you think we rarely feel like giving, even when we have an abundance?

3. Consider the two stories about the rich ruler in Luke 18 and Zacchaeus in Luke 19. How are they similar? How are they different?

God Challenges Israel
to Test His Immeasurable Generosity

Notice how God finished this section. He gave an amazing promise to His people that would be fulfilled when they obeyed His commandments. In fact, the only time in the Bible where God actually directed people to test Him in the area of finances is found in verse 10:

> "Bring the full tenth into the storehouse so that there may be food in My house. Test Me in this way," says the LORD of Hosts. "See if I will not open the floodgates of heaven and pour out a blessing for you without measure."

The temple's storehouse was filled with numerous rooms that contained grain, oil, and various other supplies for the wellbeing of the priests. It was the requirement of God that the people give money and supplies for the preservation of the Levites. God, who knows intimately the hearts of men, anticipated His people saying, "We can't give 10 percent." So God said, **"Test Me."** They thought, "We can't afford to give." God corrected them, "No, you can't afford not to give. Test Me."

The word rendered **test** can be used to refer to a number of potential acts. It can be used either positively or negatively to connote testing or challenging. A different Hebrew word, frequently translated with some variation of the word *test,* reflects an arrogant or cynical attitude at work. The word used here, however, suggests an attitude of honest doubt. The purpose of this testing is to confirm or encourage faith. God says, in essence, "Go ahead and test Me. Be obedient to Me and I will open the floodgates of blessing upon you."

The term *floodgate* is the same word used in Genesis 7:11 to describe when God opened the heavens to release the floodwaters that covered the earth. Can you picture it? God was saying that for the financial generosity of the Israelites, He would excessively pour out His blessings upon them.

But the Lord promised not only to provide for them, but also to protect them. Look at verse 11: **"I will rebuke the devourer for you, so that it will not ruin the produce of your land and your vine in your field will not fail to produce fruit,"** says the LORD of Hosts. The NIV alternatively renders this verse, "I will prevent pests from devouring your crops." The word *devourer* could refer, as it does in Jeremiah 30:16, to the destruction of Israel at the hands of a foreign army. Further, it is used in Hosea 8:14 to refer to the destructive nature of fire. So, regardless of whether the "devourer" is insects, fire, or an army, God told the Israelites, "No matter what happens to you, when you are financially faithful to Me, I will provide for you. I will protect you."

Locusts devouring a plant.

God's Blessing upon Israel will Result in a Good Reputation Among the Nations

Finally, God promised that He would make prosperous those who obey Him (v. 12): **"Then all the nations will consider you fortunate, for you will be a delightful land," says the LORD of Hosts.**

God would give them a good reputation, as He promised Abraham in Genesis 12. If the people of Israel were willing to esteem God as the highest priority in their lives, God promised to make them great. That is, if Israel exalted the name of the Lord, He would exalt their name among the nations. He would make their land a **delightful land.** This means that there would be no more need, no more rampant disease or wickedness among the people, no more war, and no more civil turmoil. There would be plenty to drink and plenty to eat. He promised to restore the land and its inhabitants, but only if they obeyed.

Conclusion: Christ as the Climax of the Covenant

What can we learn from the actions (or inactions) of Israel and the promises of God in Malachi 3:6-12? First, as with much of Malachi, we learn that if we obey the mandates of

LEARNING ACTIVITY

The Blessings of Obedience

Look at verses 10-12 and the information here in the Personal Learning Guide. How would you complete the three areas in which God promised to bless the Israelites if they would "test" Him?

1. "I will ... p_____ out a b_____ for you without m_____ " — Promise of God's P_____

2. "I will r_____ the d_____ for you" — Promise of God's P_____

3. "All the nations will c_____ you f_____ " — Promise of a Good R_____

Now, think of contemporary ways in which these same promises could apply to you and your family in today's world!

1.

2.

3.

God in humble and faithful service, we can expect God's best. This does not mean that reward is immediate, or even that we will ever receive it on this side of heaven. But we are guaranteed to experience God's blessing by walking in His statutes.

Second, we learn that what defines us is not what we have or what we think we have earned. Rather, it is what we do with the resources God has provided. No one will say when standing before the judgment throne of God, "If only I had spent more money to spend on myself!" The one focused on God's glory will say, "If only I had invested more of my money in the kingdom!" Financial activity, just like all other actions, testifies as to whether you are a kingdom-bound or hell-bound individual. Jesus said we can recognize God's own by the fruit they bear (Matt. 7:16,20).

And finally, we see in this passage and the rest of the Bible that God is once again faithful to His covenant, even when His people are not. Israel would fail again, but in Christ we see the One who gave generously of Himself, even unto death, out of obedience to His Father. Men and women may let you down, but Christ never will. And in His sacrifice He also became the generous outpouring of heavenly blessing that God bestowed on all people.

Personal Reflection:

1. Where else in the Bible is God tested? How are those times similar to and different than God's command in Malachi 3:10?

2. Read Lamentations 3:19-24 and Hebrews 13:8, and compare those messages with Malachi 3:6. What's the consistent message in all three passages?

3. What part of your attitude toward money should you change in light of this study?

CHAPTER SIX

What Have We Spoken Against You?

MALACHI 3:13–4:6

The Fear of God

The promises of God will sustain the people of God. They know whose they are, and they know whom they will serve. The promises of God will allow them to endure pain and hardship in the future.

Recently, a group of psychologists did a study and found that the number one phobia in the world is public speaking. You may relate to this finding on some level, and you'd be far from alone in that feeling. But public speaking is only one of many ways that we can be afraid, and most fear will only hinder us from being all that God has called us to be.

Worldly fear should never be in the vocabulary of a Christian. Jesus, the Prince of Peace, repeatedly spoke peace to His followers and told them not to be afraid. In fact, when Jesus rose from the dead and met the terrified disciples, He walked into the room and the first thing He said to them was, "Peace to you!" (Luke 24:36). Jesus was pulling from a long tradition set forth in the Old Testament in which the people of God were consistently met with the same reassurance in response to fearful situations: Do not be afraid.

In what seems like a stark contrast to this biblical exhortation, however, we also have passages that talk about fearing God. In the account of the thieves on the crosses next to Jesus, one thief looked to the other and said with understanding, "Don't you even fear God?" (23:40). So the question is: should we be fearful of God or not?

I will answer this question with both *yes* and *no*. We should never be afraid of God as believers, but we should always have a reverential fear of Him, an humble respect for a holy and righteous God who has given us life, and can also take away our life in the blink of an eye. God is pleased when we fear and obey Him, but those who are adopted into His family through Christ need not cower in fear of His eternal punishment. To them, He is a loving Father.

Personal Reflection:

In what sense should we fear God? What are some examples of an unhealthy fear of God?

The Wicked Respond in a Spirit of Legalism, Expecting Reward for Obedience

In Malachi 3:13-16, God set His heart on His treasured possession. God had just finished talking about money and devotion, and declared that the heart of the problem was a problem of the heart. God's grievance was not primarily with the people's finances; rather their finances were the vehicle by which God uncovered deep-rooted sin. God challenged the people to trust Him, and to see the blessings He would pour out if they would commit themselves totally to Him.

In this passage, though, God changed His tone from leniency to seriousness and divided the group addressed into two categories: those who were following Him and those who were not following Him; those who were faithful to Him and those who were separated from Him. Look at the text, starting in verse 13, taking notice of the first group:

"Your words against Me are harsh," says the LORD. Yet you ask: "What have we spoken against You?" You have said: "It is useless to serve God. What have we gained by keeping His requirements and walking mournfully before the LORD of Hosts? So now we consider the arrogant to be fortunate. Not only do those who commit wickedness prosper, they even test God and escape." (Mal. 3:13-15)

This first group included those who had strayed from God. We know they had strayed from God because of their actions. Notice their attitude towards serving the Lord: they considered it **useless.** That is a bold and dangerous attitude to have, for *useless* means vain or futile, something that is a waste of time. The people claimed they gained nothing by serving the Lord. Instead they were checking off the boxes of their religious obligation. "What are we profiting," they asked, "by keeping His commandments or mourning before the Lord of hosts?" In their hearts, they believed nothing was gained through obedience.

Their lament deepened with the inclusion of the phrase ***walking mournfully.*** In this text, *mournfully* communicates the idea of repentance. Their complaint was that they had already repented, yet God had not responded. The issue with this

mentality is that it is one of reciprocity, of feeling as if one deserves something in return for something that one has done. It is like saying, "You need to do something for us because of what we have done for you." Do we see this in the church today? Can we hear people saying, at least in attitude if not in so many words, "God, because I have done that for You, now You should do this for me"?

We can do the right thing with the wrong motive and miss the point completely, which is exactly what the people of Israel were doing. They were mindlessly following protocol in the ministry. They were filling in blanks under the header "stuff we've done for God." But what they were doing for the Lord missed the heart of what God desired.

They adopted a mentality of reciprocity not only in their actions toward the Lord, but also in their attitudes. Notice verse 15: **"So now we consider the arrogant to be fortunate. Not only do those who commit wickedness prosper, they even test God and escape."** In chapter 1, the people were saying, "God, You are blessing the unrighteous while we are floundering here as Your chosen people. You are blessing the wicked, but not the people of God. Why is this happening?" The first group in chapter 3 echoed the same concern.

What are the implications of God's Law becoming a waste of time? How does one even get to that place? It is certainly true that God's Law wasn't inherently burdensome to His people. In fact, to the Jewish mind the Law was good. They loved the Law. It lit their steps; it revealed their paths. To the people of Israel, the Law was life, similar to how Paul said in Romans 7:22, "For in my inner self I joyfully agree with God's law."

This concept is foreign to most 21st century Americans. Rather, the law is equated with policemen and speeding tickets, with courts and condemnation. No one got up this morning, jumped out of bed, and said, "I am ready to obey the laws of my state today," or, "I cannot wait to drive 55 on the interstate to church this morning!" But the people of Israel were meant to look at the Law, which was the Torah, with love. They were commanded to obey it, for it brought life. The Torah contained the words from their personal God.

The people had strayed from that love, though. What God was demonstrating here was that if we do not understand the heart of the commands, it is possible to follow them technically and still be far from God personally. Or, alternatively,

Mourning women depicted in a wall painting fragment from the tomb of Neb-Amon at Thebes. The women kneeling in the lower right of the painting are putting dust on their heads.

ILLUSTRATOR PHOTO/ DAVID ROGERS/ MUSEUM OF FINE ARTS, BOSTON (6/4/15)

we may discard them altogether. These people had strayed away in their attitudes and in their actions, and God demanded a change.

Personal Reflection:

1. How do you see Christians adopting a mentality of reciprocity when it comes to serving the Lord?

2. In what sense is the Law not a burden to God's people? How can it become burdensome?

The Righteous Respond with a Heart
of Reverent Fear, Esteeming His Name

At verse 16, the Lord switched gears. We witnessed the first group straying from God by expecting a reward for their obedience. Now, we meet a second group who served God faithfully. The most remarkable difference between this second group and the first is their attitude. We see it clearly in verse 16: **At that time** *those who feared the* Lord **spoke to one another** (emphasis added). Their attitude is the blueprint for how we should serve the Lord—with a healthy fear of God. The Book of Malachi proposes that this is a fear every believer should possess.

The concept of fear occurs many times in the Old Testament. There are three main Hebrew words that are translated as "fear." One is the Hebrew word *pachad*, which means "to be afraid, startled, or stand in awe" (Hos. 3:5). The second one is *arats*, which means "to be terrified, dread" (Isa. 29:23). The third one, *yirah* or *yare*, means "reverence or respect or awe." This third usage is the concept Malachi had in mind in this text. When aptly translated, it means a "reverential respect or awe for God."

We should never cringe in trepidation in the presence of holy God as believers. We should never shrink back from Him. We should stand humbly before God because of who He is and what He has done for us. This word *yare* or fear is used in a variety of ways: First, notice Proverbs 3:7: "Fear the LORD and turn away from evil." When we fear God, to have respect and reverential appreciation for Him, we will not be involved in evil. Second, in Deuteronomy 31:12, Moses said, "Gather the people—men, women, children, and foreigners living within your gates—so that they may listen and learn to fear the LORD your God and be careful to follow all the words of this law." This verse shows that when we fear God, we will obey Him. The third usage can be found in Proverbs 9:10, which states, "The fear of the LORD is the beginning of wisdom." When we fear God, we are endowed with godly wisdom.

When those who feared (*yare*) the Lord understood this concept, they naturally began to speak about Him to others. Possibly, they spoke about the goodness of God. Maybe they offered testimonies of His kindness and longsuffering. Maybe they were appreciative of what God had done for them. Specifics of what they talked about aren't shared, but what is evident is that fear of God will manifest itself in the proclamation of Him.

The fear of God affects both our attitude toward and our actions before Him. God does something especially awesome in return to this posture. He says, "If you fear me, I will remember you." Look at the promise in verse 16: **The LORD took notice and listened.** When the people feared the Lord, He paid attention and He heard them.

The LORD took notice and listened. So a book of remembrance was written before Him for those who feared Yahweh and had high regard for His name (v. 16). Other references to heavenly records are found in several places throughout Scripture. One is in reference to our eternal destiny. Revelation 13:8 contains the names that are written in the book of life before the foundation of the world. A second is a book that records the judgment of God against sinners, which can be found in Isaiah 34:16. The third book we know about is the one in which our sins are recorded, found in Revelation 20:12.

But Malachi's book of remembrance is quite different than these. Malachi's book isn't a book that records the wicked acts of sinful individuals or God's judgments against them. This book logs the righteous acts, deeds, and motives of God's people. Scripture clearly speaks of the fact that God doesn't miss anything. This concept was prevalent during Malachi's day. Kings and rulers frequently kept similar record books.

Whenever someone performed a favor for a king, an assistant would record it in order to return the favor in the future.

God is recording every time you respond in righteousness. Every time a woman respects her body and rejects intimacy before marriage or outside of marriage, God sees and honors it. Every time a husband rejects the temptation to engage in immoral talk, seduction, or viewing pornography, God recognizes it. Every time you refuse to entertain gossip, every time you bear the burden of an injustice and refrain from lashing out, God notices that. Every time a family builds their home to be a Christian witness to the world, God sees that. Every time you share the gospel with a lost family member, coworker, or friend, God recognizes that, whether or not anybody else does. If we lived with this in mind, how would it change the way we live?

Amazingly, verse 17 contains an allusion to the Lord Jesus: **"They will be Mine,"** says the Lord of Hosts, "a special possession on the day I am preparing. I will have compassion on them as a man has compassion on his son who serves him."** God gives two promises: They will be God's **special possession,** and He will show them mercy (not giving them the punishment they deserve). **The day** in question was the day in which Christ would come and secure His people for God's own possession once and for all through His death and resurrection. We as New Testament believers are sealed through a personal relationship with God's Son, an incredible picture of God's lasting remembrance that continues to this day.

Calling something a "special possession" is noteworthy. It is a phrase one would reserve for a collection of jewels or other treasured possession. It is used in 1 Chronicles 29:3, when David had amassed huge quantities of gold and silver for the construction of the temple, but he also made an additional offering of his personal, treasured possession. It was like the contents of his safe-deposit box in addition to his savings account.

Here it is as if God says, "To Me, you are My treasured possession," and each of us should feel the weight of that proclamation. The God of the universe looks at you as His private treasure, as the object He values highly and protects next to His heart.

Malachi said God would spare the righteous as a man spares his own son who serves him. What an amazing promise of God! God says, "I will save you not because of what you have done, for you have strayed, but because of the promise I made to your forefathers many years ago." God's memory knows no limits and His book misses no records; His record book is true and His actions are unfalteringly just.

This chapter finishes with a summary statement that wraps up the discussion of these two groups in verse 18: **So you will again see the difference between the righteous and the wicked, between one who serves God and one who does not serve Him.**

Personal Reflection:

1. How would you explain the "fear of the LORD" to an unbeliever?

2. Why do you think the Israelites' fear of the Lord led them to talk about Him (see v. 16)?

3. Is it comforting or troubling to you that the Lord keeps a record of all that is done in this life? Explain.

The Day of the Lord as a Day of Judgement

It is, perhaps, up to us to determine which of these categories we fit into. It is crucial that we figure it out, because chapter 4 comes quickly, suddenly, with its talk of judgment for those who are found in the wrong camp:

> "For indeed, the day is coming, burning like a furnace, when all the arrogant and everyone who commits wickedness will become stubble. The coming day will consume them," says the LORD of Hosts, "not leaving them root or branches. But for you who fear My name, the sun of righteousness will rise with healing in its wings, and you will go out and playfully jump like calves from the stall." (Mal. 4:1-2)

The text begins on a negative note with Israel's darkness. God is just and will judge righteously the wrongs committed against Him. Verse 1 is actually the response to the objection the people had raised earlier in 2:17, asking in essence: "Why are the wicked flourishing and we, as the faithful people of God, floundering?" God responded in 4:1: **"The day is coming."** This reminds us of the Lord's appearing. It will be a day when God Himself will show up and make all the wrongs right. God's words were encouraging and troublesome for Israel.

The Israelites were expecting a blessing. God informed them He would come **like a furnace.** By God's own mouth, He intends to cleanse and purify, not coddle. He continued, **when all the arrogant and everyone who commits wickedness will become stubble.** That word *arrogant* is another word for the prideful. A day is coming when their present pride will be squashed. Many, in their own minds, are independent of God's assistance. They have no care for Him, no need for Him. But the day of reckoning is fast approaching. God will come with recompense for their evil deeds.

Malachi reassured the people in verse 3 that God always delivers on His promises. He declares, **"You will trample the wicked, for they will be ashes under the soles of your feet on the day I am preparing."** God finally answered the question that was posed in 3:14, where the people inquired about what was gained from following the Lord. God revealed that they would experience victory over the unrighteous, though it seemed that the wicked were currently prospering.

The people of Israel were longing for the day to come when God would come down, but they did not realize the implications of His return—judgment. We know that Christ has already come, and that He is coming again. The question each one of us must ask ourselves is, "Am I ready for this second coming?"

Personal Reflection:

How does God's judgment work like a purifying furnace? Compare this with Hebrews 12:18-29.

The Dawn of the Sun and the Vindication for God's People

The Lord will bring perfect, righteous judgment when He returns, which we've realized is a curse as much as it is a blessing. Verse 2 highlights the blessing: **"But for you who fear My name, the sun of righteousness will rise with healing in its wings, and you will go out and playfully jump like calves from the stall."** Those who fear the Lord's name are the ones whose names are written in the Lamb's book of life. They will be protected from the fiery furnace, and **the sun of righteousness will rise.** This is the only occurrence of "sun of righteousness" in the entire Bible. It conveys images of a brilliant morning and the sun's rays going forth providing warmth, heat, and comfort to those under it. Malachi said that the sun of righteousness will rise also **with healing in its wings.**

This sun is not an inanimate object, but a person. It is God Himself. It is the manifest presence of God. The Hebrew word *kanaph* is here translated as "wings." It occurs elsewhere in the Old Testament to refer to a number of different things. In Genesis 1:21, it speaks of the winged animals of creation that fly around the earth. It is used in Isaiah 6:2 to describe the wings of the seraphim who worshiped God. Interestingly, it also is used to refer to the corner or the hem of a garment. In the Book of 1 Samuel, after Saul was disobedient to the Lord, the Lord sent Samuel to confront Saul and strip him of the kingdom. Saul responded by grabbing the corner or the hem *(kanaph)* of Samuel's garment so that it ripped (15:27). So Malachi said the sun of righteousness would come with healing. His coming will be so associated with the healing and restoring of His people that it is as if He would be wearing it. The sun of righteousness, God Himself, will have healing in His wings.

It was assumed in ancient Israel that the hem of the garment of righteous men contained healing properties. Yet the healing that Malachi talked about was a spiritual healing from sin and separation from the Lord. Therefore, this sun would come with jubilation and celebration. When He comes, "you will go out and playfully jump like calves from the stall." The Israelites would take the calves in the winter and put them in stalls, and they would be locked up all winter. We can imagine the calves' excitement the moment the stalls were opened up. Malachi said that the excitement of God's people over His coming will resemble this jubilation.

Remembering the Law as a Means of Sustaining Present Obedience

Next, God shifted from what He would do to those who are far from Him and spoke directly to the people of Israel.

Notice the directive in verse 4 to remember the Word of God: **"Remember the instruction of Moses My servant, the statutes and ordinances I commanded him at Horeb for all Israel."**

God closed with a call to remember the teaching of Moses, the torah. Israel was never to separate following God from following God's law, for they are one and the same. Jesus' words affirm this in Matthew 5:17: "Don't assume that I came to destroy the Law or the Prophets. I did not come to destroy but to fulfill." God has given through His Word, particularly the Old Testament, a road map for success—not riches and fame—but for pleasing Him and living the abundant life.

The Hebrew Bible, what we refer to as the Old Testament, is understood by Jews to have three sections, often collectively referred to as the *Tanakh*. Each of the consonants in this word represent one of the three sections. So the "T" stands for the *Torah*, the Law. Secondly, the "N" stands for the *Neviim* or the prophets (the main Hebrew word for prophet is *nevi*). Thirdly, the "K" is for the *Ketuvim*, or the writings. This section contains much of the wisdom literature and poetry books of the Old Testament.

The first books of the *Neviim* and the *Ketuvim*, Joshua and Psalms, each begin with a call to remember, or look back and meditate on, the Law. Joshua 1:7 reads, "be strong and very courageous to carefully observe the whole instruction My servant Moses commanded you." Psalm 1 begins similarly: "How happy is the man who does not follow the advice of the wicked .... Instead, his delight is in the LORD's instruction, and he meditates on it day and night" (vv. 1-2). Looking at the prevalence of God's Law throughout the Old Testament, it should be no surprise that God turned to the people of Israel at the end of Malachi and commanded them to remember Moses' instruction. This is consistent with what He had instructed the people to do from the very beginning of their existence!

Personal Reflection:

1. What good will come of remembering the Law of God in your life? What good does God say will come of it?

2. Review Matthew 5–7. What was Jesus' attitude toward the Law of God? How should Christians think about the specific commands of the Law?

Looking Forward in Hope, Anticipating Restoration Through the New Elijah

Malachi announced in 3:1 that the forerunner to the Messiah would come. We know from the New Testament that the forerunner was John the Baptist. But 4:5-6 indicate that there would be another person, another forerunner, to come before the day of the Lord:

Look, I am going to send you Elijah the prophet before the great and awesome Day of the LORD comes. And he will turn the hearts of fathers to their children and the hearts of children to their fathers. Otherwise, I will come and strike the land with a curse.

We know this forerunner cannot ultimately be John the Baptist because the day discussed ends with fathers turning their hearts to children and children turning their hearts to fathers. If this prophecy were completely fulfilled in John the Baptist, we might ask why Jesus was still rejected by the Jews. So what was God talking about here? Although Jesus said in Matthew 11:7-10 that John the Baptist is the forerunner, something happens in the Gospels that shows us there is yet another "Elijah" who will fulfill this prophecy in Malachi.

LEARNING ACTIVITY

Two Pillars

Read each of the following statements. Then identify whether the statement refers to Moses or Elijah.

_____ Delivered the Law of God to the Israelites
_____ Represented God during the days of King Ahab
_____ Challenged God's people to service
_____ Challenged God's people to obedience
_____ Died on the top of a mountain looking over into the promised land
_____ Was taken up to heaven in a fiery chariot
_____ Stood with Jesus at His Transfiguration

In Matthew 17, Jesus took three disciples up to the mount of transfiguration. There, both Elijah and Moses appeared and talked with the Lord.

As Jesus' face shone like light, the disciples fell to the ground and they realized who Jesus is. The disciples asked specifically about this verse in Malachi (see Matt. 17:10). Jesus replied, "'Elijah is coming and will restore everything,' He replied. 'But I tell you: Elijah has already come, and they didn't recognize him. On the contrary, they did whatever they pleased to him'" (vv. 11-12). The key phrase for our purposes is the future tense "will restore." At the time Jesus was speaking, John the Baptist was already dead. So we know that he cannot be the final fulfillment of Elijah of Malachi 4:5. In addition, this Elijah would "restore everything," and John the Baptist did not do so—the wickedness of the people's hearts remained.

Jesus will be the ultimate Elijah-like figure who would initiate His kingdom at His resurrection and will complete it at His second coming, when He will turn the hearts of fathers to their children and the hearts of children to their fathers.

The good news delivered in verse 5 was short-lived, though, for the final words of Malachi raise the prospect of a curse: "utter destruction," as the ESV says. Notice that this is the end of the final book in the Old Testament—which makes "utter destruction," or "curse" the last thing that the Israelites heard from God for some 400 years until Jesus arrived on the scene. That is a long, thought-provoking silence.

Personal Reflection:

1. How is the promise of judgment comforting in the midst of evil and injustice in the world? What specific injustices do you long to see corrected by God's judgment?

2. Discuss the identity of the forerunner in Malachi 4:5. Is this the same as or different than the forerunner in 3:1?

Conclusion: Christ as the New Elijah, the "Sun of Righteousness," and the Light of the World

Let us end with a reflection on the sun of righteousness coming with healing in its wings (or, as we learned, "garment"). In Matthew 9:20-22, we see a woman who reached out to Jesus out of complete desperation:

> Just then, a woman who had suffered from bleeding
> for 12 years approached from behind and touched
> the tassel on His robe, for she said to herself, "If I
> can just touch His robe, I'll be made well!" But Je-
> sus turned and saw her. "Have courage, daughter,"
> He said. "Your faith has made you well." And the
> woman was made well from that moment.

She knew that if she touched the hem of Jesus' garment, she would be healed. And Jesus commended her for her faith.

Matthew specifically noted that the lady reached out and touched the "tassel" on Jesus' robe. Tassels were attached to the corners of the hem of garments. I believe many of the Jews to whom Matthew wrote would have been so steeped in the Old Testament that they would have immediately known why she wanted to touch His garment and that in doing so, the woman was confessing her belief that Jesus was the sun

Man at the Western Wall in Jerusalem wearing a traditional prayer shawl with long tassels at the corners. The woman who suffered from bleeding for 12 years believed the words of Malachi when he said the Messiah would have healing in the "wings" of His robe.

ILLUSTRATOR PHOTO/ BRENT BRUCE (60/0496)

of righteousness from Malachi 4 with healing in His garment. He was, in essence, God Himself.

To confirm that Jesus was the dawning sun, we may also look to Luke 1:76-79:

And child, you will be called a prophet of the Most High, for you will go before the Lord to prepare His ways, to give His people knowledge of salvation through the forgiveness of their sins. Because of our God's merciful compassion, the Dawn from on high will visit us to shine on those who live in darkness and the shadow of death, to guide our feet into the way of peace.

In this passage, John the Baptist's father, Zechariah, had been mute for a season. When all of the sudden he was able to speak, one of the first things out of his mouth was a prophecy. He declared that John would prepare the way for "the Dawn from on high." Not surprisingly, John's ministry would be to prepare the way for Jesus Christ.

Jesus Christ is the light to our soul, "the sun of righteousness," just as the sun is light and life to the planet. Jesus Himself declared, "I am the light of the world" (John 8:12). The question for every one of us is, has that light shone in our hearts today?

Personal Reflection:

Why did God remind the people to remember His Word (Mal. 4:4)? How does this relate to the judgment and deliverance He had been talking about?

LEARNING ACTIVITY

Instruction or Warning?

In the last verses of Malachi's prophecy, he issued both instructions and a warning. Identify people (including perhaps yourself) who need to be reminded to stay faithful to God's instructions, and those who need to be warned about the direction their lives are going. Use this exercise to create a prayer list for those you identified. Pray God will remind those who need to be instructed to remain faithful and will convict those who need to be warned. Ask God to help you be His instrument in the lives of these people.